Aesthetics

of

Generosity

El Sistema,
music education,
and
social change

José Luis Hernández-Estrada

Aesthetics of Generosity:
El Sistema, music education, and social change

This is an academic contribution by a *Sistema Fellow* at the New England Conservatory for the advancement of music education for social change. This is a not-for-profit publication. Any proceeds from this book will be donated to an existing El Sistema-inspired initiative.

For comments and letters to the author please write to:
Postal Office Box 8788, Hidalgo, TX, 78557 and/or
joseherstrada@gmail.com

José Antonio Abreu's TED Prize Speech is republished under a Creative Commons license.

Cover design by Ana Alexandra Grigoriu.
www.books-design.com

All photos by the author unless noted otherwise.

ISBN-13: 978-1480227187 (CreateSpace-Assigned)
ISBN-10: 1480227188
BISAC: Music / Instruction & Study / General
10 9 8 7 6 5 4 3 2 1

For Maestro Abreu and the teachers of El Sistema:
champions of peace.

ACKNOWLEDGMENTS

WRITING THIS BOOK WAS TRULY A LABOR OF LOVE. It is also the synthesis of a year-long academic exploration and reflection on music education for social change. It could not have been possible without the support of so many of my colleagues, mentors, and friends.

I would like to thank my family for their unyielding support throughout my Fellowship year at NEC and beyond. I would also like to thank José Antonio Abreu, to whom I dedicate this book, for his generosity and ongoing mentorship. *Dear Maestro, knowing you has been one of the most inspiring opportunities of my life.* His colleagues at FundaMusical Bolívar: Rodrigo Guerrero, Eduardo Mendez, Bolivia Bottome, Rafael Elster, and many others, were always willing to share their thoughts and ideas with an openness of heart. I am in their considerable debt.

The leadership and faculty of the New England Conservatory played a most important role as well. Thank you, President Tony Woodcock and Dean Leslie Wu Foley, for your faithful support. I also appreciate the contributions of Erik Holmgren and Elisabeth Babcock; they were both wonderfully committed to opening up ample *spaces* for thoughtful reflection and inquiry. Eric Booth was such a caring and influential mentor. I learned so much from him. He was also the first person to suggest I write a book.

The Sistema Fellows program would not have been possible without the visionary support of NEC's *Friends of the Sistema Fellows Committee* and the TED organization. My colleagues from the League of American Orchestras, the LA Philharmonic, Community MusicWorks, and the Askwith Forums at the Harvard Graduate School of Education also informed my work this year. Marshall Marcus, Susan Siman, Stanford Thompson, Daniel Trahey, Benjamin Zander, Mark Churchill, Dani Bedoni, Jamie Bernstein, Suki de Braganza, and Mercedes Rodman were very kind to share their support throughout the year; and their thoughts and dreams for El Sistema. Anneli Purchase also deserves special recognition, as she provided artful feedback on my manuscript.

My colleagues from the *Sistema Fellows* program play an important role in my life. Thank you: Alysia, Avi, David, Stephanie, Jennifer, Julie, Ben, Albert, and Aisha for your enduring friendship and for sharing your many talents with me. Finally, I would like to thank Maestro Gustavo Dudamel and all of the young musicians of El Sistema whom I worked with during my residency in Venezuela—for sharing their glorious music-making and leading me to discover new realms of possibility. God bless you all.

TABLE OF CONTENTS

PRELUDE

In 1975, José Antonio Abreu, a Venezuelan economist and musician, founded El Sistema, a revolutionary music education and social action project that has changed the lives of thousands of his country's youth. Its social and artistic achievements are spellbinding. Some of its graduates have gone on to pursue musical careers outside of Venezuela. Its most famous graduate, Gustavo Dudamel, the charismatic 31 year-old music director and conductor of the Los Angeles Philharmonic, has already achieved a pre-eminent status in the world of classical music.

For all its accomplishments, El Sistema has positioned itself as an important voice in the realm of arts learning and as a powerful example of how music can affect social change. As an inspirational social action project, it has brought a myriad of artists, educators, and activists together to engage with its ideas; in hope that these might reveal new opportunities for the advancement of artistry and education in our times.

In 2009, Maestro Abreu was awarded the TED (Technology, Entertainment, and Design) Prize and was granted a wish: to identify "gifted young musicians, passionate about their art and social justice," who would take his vision to the world. Upon his recommendation, the Sistema Fellows program was established at the world-renowned New England Conservatory in Boston.

In 2011, I was invited to take part in the Fellowship and embarked on a year-long journey of artistic reflection inspired by the work of El Sistema. At the invitation of FundaMusical Bolívar, ten Fellows traveled to Venezuela and visited dozens of music learning centers across the South American country. We worked with hundreds of students, giving all of our strength to teaching *and* learning.

On our last day in Venezuela, Rodrigo Guerrero, deputy director for international affairs at El Sistema, had a special announcement to make. Maestro Abreu would host the Fellows in an official farewell meeting. "He wants to hear about your experiences," he said. The timing couldn't have been better. We had been fully immersed in the work of El Sistema—connecting with students and their teachers, families, and cultural leaders.

And yes, we had even indulged in the exquisite local foods, danced to the folk music, and savored the countryside: visiting tropical beaches, climbing the lush hills of Cubiro, or riding a cable car up to the mountains of *El Avila* to see Caracas at dusk. After five weeks, my own Spanish became flavored with a songlike Venezuelan accent.

We are to visit the maestro at his private offices in *Parque Central*, an urban office complex in downtown Caracas. Our vans will have to leave earlier than usual. It is Monday early evening and rush hour is fierce, we are told. Driving around town can be quite an experience. It is the perfect way to feel the city's vibrant pulse. Caracas is a city of many colors and contrasts. It is a very musical city too! People will roll down their car windows and blast their stereos at full volume. The aural space is clearly flanked by lots of *salsa* and *bachata*, but surprisingly, American jazz as well. Public transportation will often be packed beyond capacity with people literally overflowing from doors and windows. Politically-charged graffiti murals adorn busy pedestrian passageways. Huge commercial billboards are also part of the visual landscape. But perhaps the most dramatic sights are the *barrios* nestled amid the city's verdant hills. From afar, the makeshift homes made up of cardboard, wood, and aluminum appear as tiny pieces of a massive tapestry. They are all painted with bright fluorescent colors, but life inside these communities can be somber and uninspiring.

As we arrive in the maestro's offices, we are quickly directed to a large conference room. There are just enough chairs for the Fellows. The walls are covered with memorabilia all lined up for everyone to see. An old photograph of Leonard Bernstein at Tanglewood stands out in the brightly lit space. Undoubtedly, the most impressive object here is the maestro's Prince of Asturias Award for the Arts proclamation:

"The jury for the Prince of Asturias Award for the Arts has agreed to bestow this award to the Youth and Children's Orchestras of Venezuela, founded by Maestro José Antonio Abreu, for having combined, within a single project, the highest artistic quality and a profound ethical conviction applied for the improvement of a social reality, in accordance with a strong conviction that music has an essential educational value for the dignity of mankind."

We are about to meet with one of the most extraordinary music educators of our time. Everyone is waiting anxiously. Some of the Fellows have prepared remarks, but they will all share from the heart. As Maestro Abreu quietly entered the room, everyone stood in gratitude. The meeting was as beautiful as I had imagined it would be. In a spirit of collegiality and generosity, many stories would be told, many experiences would be shared. It is in this very same spirit that I share this book.

It is also my hope that you will be inspired by the beauty of El Sistema and enthused to join the cause of *social action through music*. As an educator, I am truly convinced that El Sistema, and its potential contributions to the development of our arts learning ecosystem, can *play* a meaningful part to advance the good work of music education and help us envision and grow innovative artistic opportunities for youngsters and communities everywhere.

This is an effort to document the work of El Sistema and to contribute a perspective to the building of a "new era in the teaching of music in which social, communal, spiritual, and vindicatory aims become a beacon and a goal for a vast social mission." This document explores El Sistema as an insightful experiment in music education—a space to act *freely* upon creative frameworks of instruction; and to practice a dynamic pedagogy of inquiry, connectedness, and empathy that influences and inspires young musicians to achieve and overcome.

In telling the narrative of my own journey as a visiting artist in Venezuela, I do not seek to define El Sistema, but rather, illustrate some of its most salient truths. This exercise is also inherently multidisciplinary. The discourse is presented as a series of thirty-two very short essays or *developing variations* (in music, the practice is formally used as composers develop a *theme* by reflecting, elaborating, and building upon it throughout the course of a piece). These writings center on El Sistema's history, philosophy, and practice. Exploring the role of *teaching and learning* is also a primary focus of this book. Teachers, in particular, may find it to be useful as they design learning experiences and ponder new habits of mind. This work was written, in part, while in Venezuela—in between rehearsals, while studying, traveling, and being surrounded by the ever-present generosity of dear friends.

BIENVENIDOS A VENEZUELA!

February 28, 2012

It's 9:30 p.m. and we have landed in Caracas. The trip from Boston to Miami and finally to our destination saw our traveling group busy at work. I brought a few scores with me. It would make sense to brush up on the Tchaikovsky symphonies before our arrival, I thought. Basking in further inspiration, some of the Fellows are reading Tricia Tunstall's book *Changing Lives*, a fascinating *reportage* on El Sistema incorporating candid observations from an American educator's viewpoint. Others are passing around Daniel Coyle's *The Talent Code*, a gripping book on the art of talent development. There is, literally, a sense of excitement in the air. No one really knows what to expect, but it already feels as if we are about to embark on a life-changing experience.

Passports in hand, the Fellows make their way into the customs checkpoint at the cavernous *Maiquetia* airport, just a few miles away from downtown. Most of them are carrying instruments: a trumpet, two violins, a viola, and a French horn. It's an odd combination for a chamber group. Given the size of our group, we look like a touring ensemble, and the immigration officer is quick to point it out. "You are an orchestra!" he exclaims.

"We are a group of musicians from Boston," I answer in Spanish.

"You know, we have many orchestras here. Hundreds! What instrument do you play?" he asked.

"I am a conductor," I reply.

He looks at me straight in the eye, and then to my relief, proudly asserts, "We have here in our country, the best young conductor in *the* world: Dudamel! Do you know him . . . ?"

"Welcome to Venezuela!" (He proceeds to stamp my passport as if giving a downbeat strong enough to summon an entire orchestra.)

It is my first trip to Venezuela. As a musician who is also a student of public policy, I cannot avoid exploring El Sistema through the lens of its native political context. (Formal explorations merit extensive research beyond the scope of what our pedagogy-centered discussion can provide. In any case, scholarly conversations stemming from examining El Sistema at the intersection of public affairs, diplomacy, and *nationalism* are as important as they are fascinating.)

El Sistema is the oldest social program in the country. It has survived a host of governments with considerably different ideologies—from that of social democrat Carlos Andrés Pérez to Hugo Chávez, a staunch proponent of a so-called *socialism for the twenty-first century*, a governing approach that seeks to eradicate the most pressing of social ailments through large-scale populist subsidies and social protection programs. Political stability in Venezuela, as in many Latin American countries, can be fragile. "It is the result of a hobbled moral deficit," some Venezuelans say. And although President Chavez's government carries a bulk of unyielding popular support, his policies have also been increasingly criticized as polarizing the country.

In the midst of it all, El Sistema, as a cultural institution, has remained faithfully apolitical. The key to its longevity has been, as noted by a Venezuelan academic, its autonomy and independence as "a policy of state and not of any particular government."

In 1979, FESNOJIV, the State Foundation for the National System of Youth and Children's Orchestras of Venezuela, was established to guide the work of social change through music in the country. El Sistema currently serves around 350,000 students who attend music learning centers across the country known as núcleos. All school-age children are welcome to attend. They receive free musical instruments and daily instruction. It is estimated that seventy percent of its participants live at or below the official poverty line. El Sistema is often referred to as the most viable option for music learning in the country. It is also an innovative model of humanist education. As a project of social development and inclusion, it brings a population of students reflecting all strata of Venezuelan society.

The global reach and artistic impact of El Sistema and its many touring orchestras is a source of national pride. Several countries around the world have developed music education programs modeled after El Sistema—England, Mexico, Brazil, and Japan, to name a few. To this day, there are more than one hundred El Sistema-inspired initiatives in North America alone, and these are growing rapidly.

In 2011, FESNOJIV was rebranded as *FundaMusical Bolívar*, retaining the spirit of its foundational charter, but now operating directly under the President's *Executive Office*. The central government, which provides upwards of ninety percent of the foundation's funding, is strongly committed to supporting the program. According to a report by the *New York Times*, the foundation's annual budget is estimated at 64 million dollars US.

For an institution of such reach and working magnitude, the numbers are unusually low, but many other local foundations, donors, and partners also contribute to the cause. As El Sistema is a responsible non-profit organization, its leaders have learned to make ends meet by being exceptionally austere. It is a cultural institution unlike any other. Most Venezuelan educators would agree that it is the closest thing to an *apostolate* in music.

An Artistic Apostolate

El Sistema is devoted to a mission consecrated to "the ethical rescue of the most vulnerable youth," as José Antonio Abreu puts it. El Sistema's founder was born in 1939 to a musical family in Valera, an industrial town often referred to as "the city of seven hills." At an early age, he learned the violin and participated as a member of an orchestra. In Caracas, he studied music education, conducting, and composition with some of the most important Venezuelan teachers of the time, including the nationalist composers Vicente Sojo and Evencio Castellanos.

It was during his university years, while studying economics at the *Universidad Católica Andrés Bello*, that he first discovered a higher calling to public service. His mentor, Fr. José María Vélaz, inculcated in him a "conscience of contribution" through reflecting upon the social problems of his country in the classroom and acting upon a responsibility to serve those less fortunate in the *barrios*. These were deeply transformative years, "a joyous process," the maestro says. He would later go on to earn a PhD in Petroleum Economics at the University of Pennsylvania. As a public officer, he has served as Minister for Culture and as a legislator in the Venezuelan Congress. His illustrious career has been intensely multi-faceted, but Maestro Abreu is first and foremost—an educator. He is also a deeply spiritual man.

His work in El Sistema, which translates as "the system," is deeply grounded upon an unfathomable sense of faith. During his many interviews and speeches, he often evokes the words of Mother Theresa, the 1979 Nobel Peace Prize laureate and champion of human rights. "The secret to being committed is faith," he says. *Prayer in action is faith. Faith in action is love; and love in action is service.* "That is where everything lies, and this is why we have faith in our work." For the same reason, he often insists that love and recognition will elevate a poor child to a place of transformation. "The most miserable and tragic thing about poverty is not the lack of bread or roof, but the feeling of being no-one, the lack of identification, the lack of public esteem."

The maestro is on an extraordinary life mission, yet he doesn't feel as if he has been chosen for anything beyond the ordinary or what might be expected of any other fellow citizen. "My mission is the same which obliges every human being: to translate my humanness to its maximum dimension." Giving through teaching is his passion. "From the minute a poor child is taught how to play an instrument, he's no longer poor," is one of the maestro's most emblematic aphorisms. It is symbolic of his pedagogical philosophy: a musical instrument to play, but also to help outline new paradigms for success in life. To fully appreciate the work of El Sistema, one must reflect upon its philosophy and practice. Maestro Abreu's transcendental artistic vision stems from a deep-seated belief in aesthetic education as a means for social progress. It is his profound understanding of the dynamics and dimension of art as a social entity that distinguishes his work from that of other educational thinkers. To deepen and inform our discussion, I shall propose these five postulates as a synthesis of Maestro Abreu's artistic philosophy:

- "Education is the synthesis of wisdom and knowledge; it is the means to strive for a more perfect, more enlightened, and more just society."
- All youngsters, without exception, should exert and consummate their right to an aesthetic education.
- Artistic projects should be conceived as *social missions.* The creative spirit intrinsic in the cause shall guide its participants to envision new personal, communal, and national realities.
- The practice of a collective, harmonious, and concerted music-making shall become an instrument for developing the "multi-dimensional capacities of the human being," thus elevating his spirit and leading him to confidence and generosity.
- "Art at the service of the most vulnerable" and as an exercise of aesthetic development transforms ethically, because "ethics and aesthetics are mutually inclusive."

THE JOURNEY BEGINS

Eduardo Mendez, the executive director of FundaMusical Bolívar, is very much against calling attention to himself. "My job is to be invisible," he tells us. "My job is to be backstage and make sure that this whole machinery works." As he describes the work of the foundation, it astounds me how much he has absorbed from his mentor's rhetoric. He speaks in both political and poetic terms with remarkable focus and ease. His three cell phones are inseparable, but they "are nothing fancy," he says.

His time is extremely limited and his job particularly multi-faceted. In his role, he must report directly to the Venezuelan President's Executive Office. In any given week, he might meet with researchers from the Inter-American Development Bank (IADB) to work on evaluation rubrics, supervise the drafting of teachers' contracts, or sign cooperation agreements with a host of working partners from around the world.

"You've already seen the film documentaries and read the newspaper articles," but let me assure you, "this will not be like the movies," he warns us. He is also quick to give us a clear-cut assessment of the national program; and tell us that we would see "very developed núcleos," but also others with "obvious scarcities and infrastructural limitations." We would also be witness to their students' spirit of generosity, he expressed. "You will notice, how they will be open to share their gifts, freely, and without prejudices. They won't feel at all intimidated by you, artists from the *revered* New England Conservatory. All of our students believe that what they do is worthy to be shared.

"When you come back to Caracas, be sure to let us know what you see, and how it can be improved. Don't be afraid to jump right in and into the action. This is how you will learn," he advised us. (The Fellows quickly internalized this advice, for wanting to be "part of the action" was never a problem.) As we are sent off, there is inevitably some fear in the group. Some of my colleagues have not traveled in Latin America before. It is a foreign space; entrenched with a different set of customs and cultural idiosyncrasies.

The ten Fellows have come armed with many questions. Why are children so excited to play music? What makes El Sistema unique among existing music education programs? What can we as educators learn from it?

Some of my colleagues have also come with particular apprehensions: that the El Sistema *magic* may not be replicable outside of Venezuela; that it might be partly a native phenomenon, part of a larger set of inimitable pedagogical assumptions and practices.

My colleagues have also brought their own perspectives and ideas to share. Everyone will focus their learning through a variety of personal lenses. Aisha Bowden, a choral director from Atlanta, will work with children's choirs to uncover the joy that emanates from the youngest of voices. David France, a violinist from Bermuda, will focus his energies on teaching as many youngsters as possible in an effort to shape and refine their playing. Albert Oppenheimer, an emerging arts administrator from Starkville, is interested in seeing and exploring as many different núcleo models as possible.

It is the third such trip that the New England Conservatory has arranged as part of the Fellowship program. In our trip alone, we are to visit over twenty different learning centers. Long before our arrival in Caracas, the Fellows had been busy learning from nationally recognized practitioners in fields as wide and diverse as strategic management, public policy, child development, and music pedagogy—all in an effort to lay frameworks to maximize learning in the field.

We are told that traveling throughout Venezuela can be tough—one must be extremely flexible and patient. Cross-country trips by car can be long and tedious; and somewhat uncomfortable by American standards. Of course, there are some security concerns as well. Venezuela, like many developing countries, is not free of the stresses of violence and crime. In the last few years, violence in Venezuela has increased severely with thousands of lives being claimed by organized crime. *El Universal*, a newspaper in Caracas, reported that 7,676 people were killed in the Caracas metro area in 2009 alone, accounting for almost one murder for every passing hour. We are to follow a strict safety protocol. We are reminded of this during a courtesy visit at the United States Embassy.

The leaders at FundaMusical Bolívar are always keen to attend to all of our needs and open to share their valuable experience with us. The Venezuelans are some of the warmest people you will ever meet. I am particularly honored by the opportunity to experience the work of El Sistema up-close-and-personal. I can't help but think of its humble beginnings. In 1975, eleven young musicians gathered in a downtown Caracas garage to rehearse with the maestro and their lives would be forever changed.

As he accepted the TED Prize, Maestro Abreu told the story of that very first meeting. "When I arrived at the rehearsal, only eleven kids had shown up, and I said to myself, 'Do I close the program or multiply these kids?' I decided to face the challenge, and on that same night, I promised those eleven children I'd turn our orchestra into one of the leading orchestras in the world." Florentino Mendoza remembered the spirit of the times as if it were yesterday. "This was a very serious matter. Here was an impeccably dressed man, showing us the future. It was the 1970s. We were living in the Woodstock era, sporting long hair, torn jeans, and ragged sandals. We thought he was crazy. How could he believe in us?"

As Eduardo recalled, that same day their maestro told them that they would be the first orchestra of many in the country and that it would travel the world as an emblem of a revolutionary music education project; that the orchestra would record the symphonies of Beethoven and Mahler for *Deutsche Grammophon*, and its sound would embody the *spirit* of Venezuela; that the world's greatest conductors would ask to work with them; and that musicians and educators from around the world would come to Venezuela and embrace the program as a treasure. "Everything has happened," Eduardo said. Pausing to take a deep breath, he remarked with a big smile on his face, "It was all true."

A SECOND HOME

The Centro Académico Infantil de Montalbán (CAIM) is one of El Sistema's flagship núcleos. It is located in a highly populated middle-class borough southwest of Caracas. It is also what the Venezuelans call a *programa modelo*, a model laboratory for teaching and learning. With a staff of over 70 teachers, the center is dedicated to perfecting El Sistema's pedagogical practices and helping youngsters achieve the highest levels of musical proficiency. Following an open-source model, educators will develop unique teaching techniques through a slow process of compilation and adaptation of best practices, which often incorporate the pedagogical ideas of Galamian, Suzuki, Dalcroze, and others.

Children as young as two years old may enroll. Early childhood education and talent development are part of the núcleo's rich curriculum. The whole program acts as a conveyor belt of opportunities. Children may continue with their studies until high school.

If they choose to pursue music professionally, they may enroll for degrees in performance and music education at the Simón Bolívar Conservatory or the *Instituto Universitario de Estudios Musicales.*

If you've been selected as a member of the National Children's Orchestra, you may come to rehearse at Montalbán during a holiday break from as remote a location as Tucupita, a city in the Orinoco River Delta, or from as close as the nearby barrio of La Sarría. World-renowned conductors often lead these sessions. Most recently, Sir Simon Rattle, the music director of the Berlin Philharmonic and a fervent supporter of El Sistema, led the National Children's Orchestra in a program featuring Mahler's *First Symphony*.

On the surface, Montalbán may seem to be El Sistema's version of an American conservatory's preparatory program, but it doesn't feel like one. Rehearsals may break into extended jam and dance sessions. The infectious rhythms of Pérez-Prado's *Mambo No. 5* are just too good to sit still. You will hardly ever see anyone practicing alone or anxious about not having made *first chair* in an orchestra. But make no mistake; the students' level of playing is impressive. Their work ethic and commitment parallels the kind of engagement stemming from a *serious* conservatory, but "this is not a school. It is a space for healthy exchange," says Rafael Elster, the academic dean of El Sistema (and a professional trumpeter with studies at Juilliard). "We cannot think of a núcleo as a conservatory. It is not rigid, not like that," he told us.

For most children here, the idea of becoming a professional musician may not even register in their list of priorities. In a rehearsal, the dynamic youngsters, some of whom are playing at a level well beyond their years, are more interested in how the Venezuelan soccer team, *"la vino tinto,"* is doing in a match against powerhouse Spain. Two boys in the back of the first violin section are clamoring for updates while their colleagues in the brass section are playing the opening of Von Suppe's *Light Cavalry Overture.*

As the orchestra is sounding, Stephanie Hsu, a Fellow from New York with a *Flipcam* on hand, is taking a guided tour of the núcleo. Three young girls with bubbly personalities are showing her around. "Here are the practice rooms," "the babies are having their lessons here," "oh, and that's the director's office. You don't want to be summoned there!" They are proud to show-and-tell. The núcleo is like a second home to them. They spend most of their free time here. One of their friends, a raucous boy with spiked hair and a bright orange T-shirt, is amused at the girls' fledging enthusiasm. He's joined our group and is more than happy to have become the center of attention.

Núcleos feel like sacred spaces—sanctuaries for the teaching and learning of music. How does this manifest itself? For one, the sheer power of sound is literally all around you. Upstairs, an orchestra of middle-school students can be working on Handel's *Water Music* while a children's orchestra plays an arrangement of Beethoven's *Ode to Joy*. Downstairs, a wind band perfects excerpts of Tchaikovsky's symphonies. In an overcrowded room next door, *cuatro* lessons (a guitar-like folk instrument) are being taught to a few dozen flute and clarinet players. Other students are taking lessons in *lenguaje musical*, an in-house curriculum that centers on elementary theory and aural skills. Children as young as three years old are working on *Dalcroze* (music and movement) exercises.

The Sheetrock walls that divide the classrooms are too thin to prevent the sounds from bleeding out. One can hear music emanate from every classroom and carry into another, creating a kaleidoscope of meshed sounds. Every student in the núcleo is aware of each other's musical activities. They can feel music as part of something larger than themselves. The experience of being *inside* a realm of music, to many, is endearing, yet almost indescribable. They instinctively know that music can offer the kind of intrinsic hope and motivation that few other activities can provide. There is a healthy seriousness about the work at hand, but above all, an extraordinary feeling of joy and devotion for music and for the community that helps create it.

As we continue our exploration, Rodrigo Guerrero, our international liaison, reminds me that El Sistema has a strong culture of visiting artists, often bringing some of the world's greatest musicians to work with the youngsters. Eduardo Mata, the late Mexican conductor and former music director of the Dallas Symphony Orchestra, was one of the first international artists to be enamored of El Sistema; traveling throughout the country, collaborating extensively with the Venezuelan orchestras, and generating some very fine recordings of Latin American masterworks for *Dorian*, a major record label. For him, El Sistema was the perfect vehicle to redirect life trajectories and transform the "sociological profiles" of youngsters in developing countries. Claudio Abbado, the celebrated Italian conductor, has also been in Venezuela to share his musical gifts and help "the system" grow. He was quick to praise the program's "impressive artistic level," and its ability to integrate a compelling "social, humanitarian, and cultural focus."

Most guests and observers of El Sistema are often captivated by the technical quality of the young musicians' playing, the focus and rigor that they bring to their music, and the *joy* that illuminates everything they do. The sheer passion that emanates from their music-making is a treasure to behold.

There is plenty of excitement in and around the núcleo, but the lively force of such inspired energy can be chaotic sometimes. I suspect someone must be really paying attention to balancing the impulse of such a vibrant space.

Zobeya Marquez, a cellist and the núcleo's assistant director, always keeps a notepad and a walkie-talkie on hand. Her attention is in many places at once. She'll be sure that class schedules are planned and executed accordingly; and will guide volunteer parents as they help supervise students and safeguard the núcleo. She'll see to that all participants feel welcome and appreciated. As a group of spirited children congregate around her to ask questions, she points us to the laminated press clippings and old concert photographs that adorn the hallways—a reminder of what has been accomplished thus far and where their students might be headed in the future. The headlines are an inspiration to all: *"Children's Orchestra Travels to Europe," "Young Musicians Captivate Sir Simon Rattle," "The Children's Orchestra: A Role Model for the Future."*

As Zobeya continues to share her day-to-day activities and responsibilities with us, she remains steadfastly watchful of her students. There are a few hundred, and every one of them "must be cared for." As they play for us in a series of showcases, she listens and approves of her students' performances. Her quiet demeanor exudes an air of solemnity, and she smiles frequently, especially as she introduces yet another performing group.

ANABEL'S MAGIC

Anabel Astudillo is working with a string orchestra of about 60 beginner students all jam-packed in a room. It would be almost unthinkable that anyone could be capable of garnering the attention of so many small children, but somehow, it works. The elementary-age children, realizing there is an international audience in the room, quickly correct their sitting posture and appear as well-behaved as they possibly can. "They aren't usually like that," a volunteer teacher says. "They are honoring the fact that visitors are here . . . you should come more often!"

Anabel's presence is *commanding* yet inviting. As they get ready to play, she instructs the orchestra to begin, "*Uno-dos-tres, can-tando!*" The children will place their bows on the D-string with spine-chilling precision. As they play, they focus their attention on producing a deep sound. Their sound is characteristically *Bolívar-esque*. With so many kids playing together in synchronicity, their orchestra resembles somewhat of a surface wave. It is a captivating scene.

"We are building a unique *culture* of sound," Anabel tells me. They are playing *open* strings accompanied by a pianist who provides a rich harmonic support. Most of the time, they are playing *martelé*, holding the bow against the string with lots of added pressure. It is an arresting sound, often lovingly referred to as Abreu's *chasquido*, the Spanish word for snap. Anabel directs her students with motherly instincts. She makes them all feel included and valued. As the lesson unfolds, they begin to reveal many of El Sistema's pedagogical virtues.

"The children are now going to play a rendition of Offenbach's theme from *Orpheus*," Anabel announces. She has asked her students for their undivided attention. With instruments on their laps, the piano sounds in the background and the group quickly breaks into the festive tune. They are singing in *solfege*—reciting note names with nimble facility. It seems very natural to them (what might be a nightmare for a college freshman taking ear-training, is but a fun game for these children). Some of the students have trouble keeping up a steady tempo. They want to go faster, often pushing the pianist into a frenzy. All but one will end the piece together. With a split-second difference, a girl with a glittery diadem sitting in the back row shouts, "Re!" It is a confident contribution but not quite in the right place. Everyone turns to her tenderly. She chuckles, and then smiles.

"It's OK to make mistakes, but let's try it again. It has to be perfect!" their teacher says.

As they get ready to move on to their instruments, Anabel leads them in a start-up ritual. "You will now play it, and sing it!" She repeats the instruction again, now with a more undulated cadence in her voice. "You will now . . . play it . . . and. . . sing it! And if I am not satisfied with the result, we will have to do it again . . . but, I know it will be great!" Off they go, and it's much louder this time around.

The lessons are multi-dimensional, incorporating a variety of moods and episodes. Every exercise is seen as an opportunity to focus on technique, theory, and expression. The three appear to be seamlessly connected. Building discipline is also a major focus here.

"OK, everyone, let's get ready!" Anabel, who has upped her energy at this stage, would go through five steps inviting students to sit up straight, ready their instrument, hold it comfortably on their chin rest, lift up their bow, and place it gracefully on the string. "I want to see the difference between the short notes and the long notes. The short are really short, and the long are really . . . ?"

"Long!" the children shouted.

As we wrapped up our busy day, Rafael Elster, our ebullient guide and fellow teacher, also left the Fellows with an important lesson: "I am sure you can already see that El Sistema is very hard work, but don't forget, one has to make it *personal* or else our mission would never work." And he is right. For teachers here, their work is without a doubt, "the most important thing in the world."

POSSIBILITY

A ten-year-old cellist approached me and unassumingly said, "*El Maestro* wants us to learn and play *la cuarta* by the end of the month."

Puzzled, I asked, "Which fourth?"

"Tchaikovsky's Fourth," he said.

I learned that just a few weeks earlier, Maestro Abreu had invited the Montalbán Children's Orchestra to play the last movement of Tchaikovsky's *Fourth Symphony* in a showcase for members of the Los Angeles Philharmonic (who were in Caracas to perform in a series of concerts). The children, all between the ages of eight and twelve, joined a massive orchestra made up of fellow students from neighboring núcleos. They played the symphony's rousing finale—by heart. It was a powerful performance, full of energy and passion, but "not quite there yet" to the standards of what the more experienced El Sistema orchestras might be able to produce.

Tchaikovsky's Fourth is an enormous task, *"un reto enorme,"* the young cellist tells me. I couldn't agree more, it is one of the most challenging pieces in the orchestral repertoire. There are many technically difficult passages in the score. Even seasoned professional orchestras struggle with the piece. But that doesn't deter the youngsters in the núcleo from wanting to learn all of the movements. They even seem to indulge in the challenge.

I read through the first movement with the students. A working rehearsal, their playing wasn't note perfect, yet filled with yearning. Through their playing, the young musicians were telling me how *hungry* they were to learn this music. The cello section, in particular, was the most engaged—all swaying to the inner pulse of the music and playing with lots of dramatic flair. They were leaning and gesturing to each other as they played, as if wanting to reach for each other's sound and incorporate it to their own. "Your performance will be incredible. What a gift you've given me," I told them.

In his survey on motivation and achievement of adolescent musicians, Matthew D. Schatt found that as a psychological construct, "motivation is considered both a catalyst for learning and an outcome of learning." In El Sistema, artistic endeavors are seen in the context of how they may help youngsters build a powerful tenacity; and because classical music is one of the most demanding of all the art forms, it is the perfect vehicle to achieve the mission.

An eleven-year-old French horn player and student in the orchestra also told me of his dream of playing the *obbligato* solo in Mahler's *Fifth Symphony*, one of the pinnacles of the orchestral repertoire. A determined young man, he has already envisioned himself on stage "in dialogue with the orchestra" and "sounding beautiful," he said. By imagining his own success, he has already placed himself on the right path to achievement. And he is not alone, because he has caring mentors who will guide him through rehearsals and constantly remind him that "discipline and hard work" will make those dreams come true. Inviting students to *believe* in themselves has to be an educator's most important priority and greatest calling.

A Social Need

A student's enrollment in a núcleo is never subject to passing an audition. The only prerequisite for admission is a desire to be *transformed through music*, or as Lila Vivas, the charismatic concertmaster of the Teresa Carreño Youth Orchestra would attest—a calling to excel. "If you have the vocation to be here . . . you'll get in. All you have to do is share your music with us." It is as simple as that.

Reflecting on the idea of inclusion, a program director told the Fellows that the doors of his núcleo would always be open to every student, without exception. He even went as far as to say that it didn't matter if they were criminals or had killed someone. "We have eternal forgiveness. . . I'll still take them too! It is our duty. The worst they are, the better!" A zealous violin teacher was equally emphatic. "I want to rescue those children, kidnap them from the streets, take them to a world of art, to a world of beauty," she said. This may all sound overtly romantic or idealistic, but we have to remember that El Sistema is not just an artistic program, but one that seeks to re-imagine music as a catalyst for social transformation. (An idea that is quickly gaining traction among music educators outside of Venezuela.)

How is a new núcleo born? Who calls for an orchestra program to launch in towns or villages that may not have one in place yet? I am told it begins with the community itself. It is a model built upon precepts of pluralism. Rodrigo Guerrero explained that nowadays núcleos have begun to sprout almost organically. The growth of programs has risen dramatically, prompting their national budget to increase by almost twenty-five percent annually since the year 2000. Communities have now begun to see music as part of something larger. Because of its transcendence and relevance, "the act of music-making is seen not only as an aesthetic need but a social need as well," he said.

When I think of orchestras, I ponder Maestro Abreu's seminal idea that as artistic structures, they can also act as microcosms of "model societies." Through orchestral practice, musicians may come to assemble their own disparate views into one that is more consistent with the needs and intentions of all participants. While the music *sounds*, the musicians must adapt to shifting dynamics and tempi; and most importantly, balance the profusion of each other's contributions. This is part of what makes an interpretation a sublime experience to behold—an example of how people can learn to work together in pursuit of common goals. As a society, we can all benefit from examining the extra-musical virtues of such a noble entity.

In Venezuela, youth orchestras have been found to enhance the fabric of communities and their quality of life. In

2007, the Inter-American Development Bank conducted a cost-benefit analysis on the social impact of El Sistema. The assessment demonstrated gains for students in aspects of civic engagement, affirming that 60.1% of participants were involved in community activities, compared to 37.9% of non-Sistema participants. Youngsters in the "validation study" also demonstrated fewer behavior problems in school, as the guardians of 12.4% of participants were notified of behavior problems, compared to 22.5% of non-Sistema participants. Overall, the researchers concluded that El Sistema promotes "a high level of psychosocial development, self-esteem, optimism, and hope" among its many constituents.

Given the relevance of El Sistema's social programming, FundaMusical Bolívar will receive funding requests from communities all around the country (almost on a daily basis). Eventually, all of them will be responded to accordingly. The foundation will supply teachers' salaries, but local programs will often have to find a suitable rehearsal venue, and in some cases fundraise for instruments, miscellaneous expenses, and other needs as well.

And while the main foundation in Caracas provides for the majority of managerial and/or artistic guidance, the programs are not wholly dependent on its patronage. As a moderator of a healthy civil society, El Sistema encourages all participants to take charge. Communities will have complete autonomy over their núcleos and the mandate to engage in dynamic conversations to determine their own fates. The national leadership will attend to their needs, but will let them act on their own accord.

PASSION FIRST

We've made it to Núcleo Sarría, an after-school El Sistema program nestled amid one of Caracas' most dangerous *barrios*. It began in 1999 as a joint pilot project of El Sistema and the Ministry of Education. Housed at the José Martí Elementary School, the núcleo serves a few hundred students from the school and other children from the community-at-large. As soon as we arrive, I am summoned to the podium.

Over a hundred children are sitting in the orchestra. As we begin Manuel Artes' lively *Chamambo*, an opening brass fanfare signals the first and second violins to begin playing their parts. As they play, they are moving back and forth to the groove of the music. The cellists to my right are smiling, then suddenly, the whole orchestra erupts in an energetic shout: "Mambo!"

The scene quickly breaks into a blissful dance: trumpet players are twirling their instruments, a bassoon player is parading across the room; the percussionists are having fun playing *fortissimo*. Everyone is cheering. The orchestra has turned into a full blown, Texas style, marching band. I had never felt such tremendous energy. And my goodness, I thought, if this is a rehearsal, imagine the performance! The group was true to the original Greek definition of an orchestra: as "the dancing place" with the suffix *-tra* denoting place and *orkheisthai* to dance. What a joy!

In Sarría, most rehearsals will turn into performances. The orchestras will play in front of audiences as much as possible—in showcases for visitors and weekly informal concerts. This reduces the pressures of a formal performance and allows musicians to focus their energies on expressing music with such joyous freedom.

I've heard from fellow conductors in El Sistema that, more often than not, their attention will be focused on helping students find *meaning* in the music they play. In Venezuela, the philosophy is often referred to as the "passion first and/or refinement second" approach. El Sistema inspired practitioners must be careful not to interpret it as passion at the expense of technique, but as "technique being an outgrowth of musical expression" (in the manner that James Mursell, the music education scholar, might have argued).

In the documentary film, *El Sistema: Music to Change Life,* a charismatic núcleo director from Maracay speaks eloquently on getting students to play with passion. "Our system puts a lot of emphasis on the idea that the children really feel the music; that they *live* the music they play. It is not about perfect playing [at first]—if they get the bowing wrong, it is fine, no problem. We say . . . feel the music . . . your technique will improve with time, but let the music live and breathe." Educators will focus on the Romantic repertoire, pieces with "a big sound," says Luis Rodriguez, a symphonic band conductor. There is a clear pedagogical intent behind the idea. "We must introduce emotion first. They [the students] must be enraptured by the lushness of sound. Only then, we can start working," he told me.

Modeling musical involvement is crucial to motivating students into tapping their expressive energies. My colleague Joshua Dos Santos, a graduate of El Sistema and a resident conductor of orchestras throughout Venezuela, has a unique approach to the rehearsal process. In his use of metaphor and story, he brings the music closer to the imagination of his students. As he is conducting, he is also actively participating: singing, demonstrating musical passages on the cello, and even playing alongside the percussion section. This kind of involvement, beyond traditional baton technique, is a trademark of El Sistema conductors, and part of the reason students can readily identify with music and its narratives.

Susan Siman, an El Sistema founding teacher, embodies these same ideals in profound ways. I first met her in Los Angeles, as she demonstrated a lesson for a group of educators at the Los Angeles Philharmonic's first international El Sistema symposium, *Composing Change*. It was a joy to witness her teaching. As she worked with a chamber orchestra made up of students from YOLA's Expo Center program, a núcleo the LA Phil built with the local and nationally renowned Harmony Project, she was quick to achieve dramatic results. As the orchestra first began playing timidly, she immediately jumped in and demonstrated with her instrument: "You see, you have to use the whole bow, we need a big sound. I know you can do it. I don't take a shy sound for an answer!"

Her animated gestures can fill up an entire room and make you feel that you are part of the action as well. If a student is not producing the *energy* or results she wants to hear, she'll direct her trust onto him, "You take the lead now. Move us forward!" They were playing *Gipsy Overture,* an early intermediate arrangement by Isaac Merle which is played obsessively by children's orchestras in Venezuela. It is an exciting piece of music, with many tempo changes, episodes, and opportunities to play with enthusiasm. After just a few minutes, the piece was already sounding more articulated, and yes, bursting "with passion!" As the children played the final chords and propelled their bows up in the air to finish off the piece, the audience jumped and cheered. It was a perfect picture.

There is *magic* in teachers recognizing every child as an asset; and making their students feel proud about making joyous music. As a teacher, one must continually be evolving, thinking ahead, and being on the cusp of the *avant-garde.* In teaching music, passion must always come first.

A COMMUNITY OF PRACTICE

If one could distill the essence of El Sistema orchestras with a single statement, it would be this: *Everyone* is a team player.

A space where competition is non-primordial is ideal for El Sistema orchestras. Hence the reason you will often find a stronger player sitting side-by-side supporting a weaker player. "If a student knows five notes, she can teach a student who only knows two," the Venezuelans say. This idea, analogous to an *apprentice* model, is important to consider. It also brings me back to my childhood chamber music lessons where my teachers would have me play Mozart *Sonatas for Four Hands*, or Mendelssohn *Piano Trios* alongside older and more experienced musicians. Or even as I practiced tennis with players ranked much higher than me.

My colleague Christine Witkowski, a member of the inaugural class of Sistema Fellows and now a núcleo director with the Los Angeles based "YOLA at HOLA" initiative, recalled in her blog the experience of sitting through auditions and playing in a rehearsal to prepare the National Children's Orchestra of Venezuela to play Mahler's *First Symphony*.

She noted that at the audition, the majority of students, many of them under ten years old, could hardly play their assigned excerpts. But as she played with them in their rehearsal, they were able to pull through and play with ease. "There was no way these students were ready to play the music, and yet, they did!" she wrote. They were in full immersion mode, they had found a way to channel the section's energy and focus it as their own. The "jitters of playing alone" in an audition were now mitigated by the strength of their collective music-making. Christine's observations prompt me to consider platforms to enhance cooperative artistic experiences.

As *communities of practice*, a sociological term coined by anthropologist Etienne Wenger, orchestras have the potential to act as living curriculums to forge "mastery and cooperative orientations, rather than competitive or ego orientations." For educators, in El Sistema-inspired domains and elsewhere, embracing this idea could be most helpful as they design innovative teaching and learning experiences. Following Wenger's framework, an orchestra conductor might seek to solve a musical problem and will ask for the musicians' direct input: "On this phrase, the articulation should match the strings, how can the woodwinds produce a similar gesture?"

Students might want to share useful information: "I have already worked on the fingerings for the Beethoven. Take a look and see what you think."

A whole section might want to agree on a particular sound texture: "Can we agree on a single bow stroke for that passage? It could be more effective that way."

Musicians might want to seek help from others: "I am having trouble hitting that high note on my trumpet. Can you show me *how* you do it?"

Given the pragmatism of these *learning* associations, an orchestra may teach students lessons that extend well beyond a life in music. By signing up for the experience of playing in harmony with others, students will come to know their orchestras as a safe-haven to learn, socialize, and feel valued. In the process, they will come to embody a spirit of solidarity.

On the subject of music education and the value of co-operative learning and artistic experiences, scholars from Cambridge University uncovered that "engaging in regular music-based activities with others (including working in ensembles and developing simple rhythmic exercises together) can conspicuously advance empathy development." In a year-long study, researchers examined interactions and relationships between students as they performed musical activities believed to promote *emotional affinities* or a "shared intentionality" between them. These included: imitation of musical *motifs*, fostering entrainment (or "synchronizing to external rhythms in the context of social interaction"), and engaging in music composition projects. On the results of the research, Ian Cross pointed out that "conventional primary music education is thought of as skill or craft based, but in the context of a musical interaction program . . . it's not just learning to do something—it's learning to interact with others." Lead researcher Tal-Chen Rabinowitch also noted that "the ability to empathize may lead to altruistic behavior." Such remarkable contributions to our understanding of music education in the context of a social experience will not only help shape the future of our art form, but will also illuminate new and important avenues to ascertain the value of artistic endeavors in significant ways. These perspectives could also positively affect domains outside the arts experience such as health promotion and wellness. The aforementioned scholars are also exploring this possibility.

Indeed, learning to interact with others while nurturing a spirit of altruism can lead us to make a more joyful music. It seems to me that students in El Sistema thrive and elaborate on this ideal. Their music-making often appears to be increasingly *tuned* to meeting each voice and instrumentalist at the nexus of their needs and aspirations. This became even clearer in Montalbán as I heard a teacher explain that their sole goal was to create a space of empathy among students, "where the older students are helping the youngest, and in turn, the latter aspire to be like their older brothers. This is where all the good things in El Sistema stem from." I couldn't agree more.

SOCIAL ACTION

"Here, among notes of harmony and hope, our youth will build the good nation that Simón Bolívar dreamt."

It's the Center for Social Action through Music, known to students nationwide as *La Sede*. El Sistema's brand new flagship learning center is a closely guarded space. There is heavy security all around the perimeter and inside of the building. I am not surprised, for the country's top young musicians practice and perform here. It was officially inaugurated on the 36th anniversary of El Sistema.

It is an architectural beauty—an aesthetically pleasing and highly functional space. At the express wishes of Maestro Abreu, there were no administrative offices built here. Everything relates to the teaching and learning of music. Soundproof practice rooms form a carefully traced maze on the fourth floor. The basement holds acoustically designed rehearsal spaces for large orchestras. A substantial library of music scores and video documentaries is available for anyone to explore. Every single performance here is documented for posterity. In an effort to promote other creative pursuits, there are rooms filled with brand new iMacs loaded with the latest sound editing and music composition software. The Simón Bolívar Concert Hall, which sits at the heart of it all, holds concerts almost daily, and they are free (Patrons will line up in the outside foyer. Everyone is guaranteed a seat until capacity is reached). The place feels like a sort of musical *mecca.* It is a very special place for many aspiring young musicians.

As we entered the space, I was immediately drawn to a massive sculpture by Jesus Soto, a *kinetic* piece made up of a few hundred strands of thin metal rods that hang from a ceiling a couple floors above. The rods, as if to engage in a dialogue with the observer, sway intermittently as light thrusts of wind seep into the open-air building. The Soto is not the only piece that lives at La Sede. There is another equally mesmerizing work by Carlos Cruz-Diez, a fellow Venezuelan kinetic artist. His piece, *Ambientación de Color Aditivo*, is a collection of colorful synthetic tiles pressed onto the walkway that leads to the Simón Bolívar concert hall. Although it relies on the movement of the viewer rather than the movement of the art object itself, the piece functions in the same spirit as the Soto. Cruz-Diez uses the so-called *moiré* effect, superimposing similar color patterns and lines to produce a feeling of motion relative to the position and interaction of the viewer.

These two works of art thrive on the idea that its observers and their environment will *awaken* a multiplicity of meanings, thus stimulating a space of harmonic equilibrium.

What better example to describe the concept of social action than examining the playful dynamics of kinetic art? Max Weber, the eminent sociologist explains that any action is deemed social to the extent that individuals are taken into account, and that in effect, will influence its outcome.

We can come to articulate the theory in more practical terms by asking the question: What opportunities may emerge from working in a spirit of reciprocity? One of the most fascinating aspects of my own art form is how people can come to relate through the experience of listening to or performing music together. Part of the aesthetics of El Sistema stem from realizing significant communal connections through narratives of solidarity. How does music help us create such bonding experiences?

When individual musicians participate in a space of musical exchange, a choir for example, they must learn to balance the texture and color of their own voices with that of the others to create a seamlessly integrated product. One with an inimitable personality, derived from the contributions of the choir as a whole.

As a performing artist, I can attest to the feeling of wholeness that this generates. When musicians generate sound and that same sound is shaped by the contributions of others, its *affect* changes. It is no longer an isolated event, no longer an isolated idea. As a result, a musical experience becomes magnified, and because music is host to sublime human virtues, the properties of these agreeable dynamics may translate into more meaningful human connections. Therein inhabits the spirit of social action. From many we are one: *E Pluribus Unum.*

THE BOLÍVARS

On a balmy Sunday afternoon, a few hundred young musicians from núcleos throughout the city were invited to
listen in to *Deutsche Grammophon's* recording session of
the Simón Bolívar Symphony Orchestra of Venezuela (often referred to in the English-speaking press as the *Bolívars*). In Venezuela, the name *Simón Bolívar* can evoke
strong feelings of patriotism. Bolívar, who is known as *El
Libertador* or "The Liberator," led Latin America's successful independence struggle against the Spanish Empire. His
words are often quoted by children and youngsters in
schools, "An uneducated being is an incomplete citizen."

Sitting in the front rows, the children all seemed to
have been enthralled by the orchestra's deep and powerful sounds. As their fiery conductor came down upon the
first chord of Beethoven's *Egmont Overture*, some children in the third row were caught jumping off their seats.
As they quickly realized the red light that was placed next
to the podium was on (a sign that the recording was ongoing) they would silently gesture to each other, "Hush!

They are recording." It was moving to see them all there, at such an important and historic occasion—listening to and embracing the music—witnessing their musical heroes.

Over the years, the orchestra has grown to develop a unique personality and charisma. It is one of the world's most exceptional ensembles—the unsurpassable artistic emblem of El Sistema. They are the heirs of the now legendary eleven young musicians that first gathered to play in a downtown Caracas garage. Since 1999, and with Gustavo Dudamel at the helm, it has gone on to perform in some of the world's most revered musical venues: the Mariinsky Theatre in St. Petersburg, the Royal Albert Hall in London, the Palacio de Bellas Artes in Mexico City, and New York's Carnegie Hall. Theirs is a rare kind of artistry. The *Bolívars* have been playing together for over a decade. They first came together to play as a children's orchestra. That orchestra grew to a youth orchestra, and now, a fully professional ensemble. There is chemistry between the musicians and their conductor that radiates a special, almost spiritual energy. You can hear it in the sound that they produce. It is a sound filled with optimism. Many children aspire to be in Dudamel's orchestra. "Landing a spot there may be the equivalent of making the roster for the Olympic team," a young musician told me.

It is fascinating to see (and hear) how European music becomes re-imagined and invigorated through the artistic lens of Venezuelan youths, making their performances an example for other youth and even professional orchestras to emulate—giving Beethoven, Mahler, or Strauss fresh and universally respected perspectives. For Latin America, this is an artistic triumph without precedent and beyond proportions; and the *Bolívars* know it's real when the London-based journal, *The Guardian,* reports that "everything they do makes European and North American ways of dealing with classical music seem grey and dull."

The Spanish poet, Juan Antonio González, is vehemently insistent, as he refers to the orchestra as a "rampaging youth that enlivens the pompous and sometimes dusty Western-developed symphonic world." For Maestro Abreu's young musicians, these reviews are a source of pride, but also a testament to their responsibility to uphold the "lofty testimony of a continent that is truly finding an upright paradigm."

I first heard news of the orchestra in 2007. Gustavo Dudamel had recently won the *First Gustav Mahler Conducting Competition* in Bamberg and the Bolívars were still known as a "youth" orchestra. I was studying at the *Conservatori del Liceu* in Barcelona when I received an e-mail with a link to a *New York Times* feature announcing an upcoming tour. Maestro Abreu and his orchestra were traveling to Mexico for the first time since 1976. I booked a ticket and flew back home to hear the prodigious musicians' Mexican debut in Monterrey.

Their interpretations of Beethoven, Bernstein, and Revueltas were intensely rich and satisfying, but their encores truly lit up the audience. Leonard Bernstein's sizzling *Mambo* from West Side Story turned into an extravagant *fiesta* with musicians dancing onstage. Arturo Marquez's sensuous *Danzón No. 2* had the solo clarinetist put a rousing spell upon the hall. To finish off the concert, Alberto Ginastera's *Malambo* from the Suite Estancia propelled a spectacle of multicolored national track jackets being thrown upwards and towards the audience (the same outfits that Venezuelan athletes often wear in competition).

It was clear that their performance involved a lot more than music itself. It had everything to do with joy. It was about feeling proud of being a musician. Here were two hundred of my colleagues overflowing with energy and conveying a powerful message: *Music is part of our lives and that is why we celebrate being alive.* I saw an indelible joy in their faces and heard it in their music too. Five years later, my memory still gravitates towards that hallowed moment. It has been a constant reminder that music can evoke powerful experiences.

After intermission, it was time for Beethoven's *Eroica*. Dudamel and his band were playing *a la Mahler*, employing as many musicians as possible, making Beethoven's music larger than life—as it should be. The *Eroica* is a revolutionary work of art. Dubbed as one of the greatest symphonies (if not the greatest) of all time, the first movement alone is longer than any complete symphony of Haydn or Mozart. Beethoven had originally dedicated the symphony to Napoleon Bonaparte, but later scratched out his name from the score, when he declared himself Emperor.

The *Bolívars* have made a case for being an orchestra with a particular aptitude for the works of Beethoven. The music of the great German composer is always about man "fighting for his destiny," says Gustavo Dudamel. Many of the youngsters in El Sistema know exactly what that means. They are *tocando y luchando*, for their own lives in the *barrios* and in the poorest of rural towns, engaging music as a way to overcome the perils of poverty.

As a source of infinite opportunity, art has the potential to propel humanity to a place of transformation and out of the confines of conformism and mediocrity. By giving us a most finished performance, beautiful in every possible way, the *Bolívars* were postulating the very essence of their artistic mission. And their music took on a much larger relevance, because it was made manifest in the hopefulness of their audience. El Sistema's pedagogical notion of *being, and not yet being*—that push-and-pull between idealism and struggle—is also very much present in the Beethoven score. And not only were the Bolívars playing it with impetus, but were also negotiating its meaning.

During the performance, one could readily feel the *Eroica's* sense of angst and despair; of heroism and possibility. Gustavo Dudamel and his orchestra would take on the role of heroes, relating the magnanimous stories to us all, and communicating a message of strength and opportunity to the young audiences at *La Sede*. The youngsters here were hanging on every note, as if they had also been playing the *Eroica*; recognizing themselves in the image of their *older* brothers and in the highest degree of artistic possibility.

After the concert, I thanked Maestro Abreu for that same gift—for inviting me to celebrate, alongside his students, the many and bountiful promises inherent in a spirit of triumph. The Fellows will now be on their way to Barquisimeto, Dudamel's hometown. He asked if he could come with us. Perhaps next time, he is reminded. His concert schedule is already packed.

A New School of
Social Life

In Barquisimeto, the "musical capital of Venezuela," I sat down for a long conversation with Maestro Luis Giménez, a founding member of El Sistema and one of its most devoted advocates. "We are living a dream," he said. And rightly so, his núcleo, now hosted at the Vicente Emilio Sojo Conservatory, was one of the first in the country. This is also where Gustavo Dudamel first picked up the baton.

The program serves about three thousand beneficiaries making up nine youth orchestras, numerous choirs, and special-needs education ensembles. I asked Maestro Giménez what had made him decide to dedicate a life to teaching music for social change. "From the very beginning Maestro Abreu had a broad vision. In 1975, when we started the *first* truly national orchestra of Venezuelans, he was already thinking about a movement. I was in the cello section. During our rehearsals, he cultivated a way of forward thinking; he was always planting seeds and sharing plans for the future." The model that the orchestra had built in Caracas was meant to be replicated. Many musicians would begin plans to build similar programs all over the country. "This wasn't just an orchestra. It was a group of individuals who would lead change in meaningful ways. First in Maracay, then in Barquisimeto, and now around the world. That's why you are here, right?" he asked.

Clearly, the orchestra has been the framework from which El Sistema has evolved. It guides the pedagogy and all social aspects of music-making. Students won't ask where you are from, but rather, what orchestra you play in. Students *love* their orchestras. For that same reason, you may find children playing side-by-side between rehearsals as duos or trios to perfect a technically demanding part. Or teenage musicians at the *areperia* (a local restaurant) during lunch hour, trying to make sense of a tricky rhythmic pattern, scores in hand, in preparation for a forthcoming rehearsal.

The orchestra is the conduit for learning and measuring achievement. In Barquisimeto, all orchestras lead to another in a pyramid scheme culminating in the Orquesta Sinfónica Juvenil de Lara, a semi-professional orchestra that can play works as complex as Prokofiev's *Fifth Symphony.* There is ample room for everyone to grow. Students transfer to advancing ensembles when they are ready, no matter the age (a twelve-year-old virtuoso is already playing the Prokofiev). Many of them spend about ten years participating in the program. The majority of graduates do not become professional musicians, yet go on to pursue other careers—doctors and lawyers being the most popular professions.

Maestro Giménez asked me to work with the Orquesta Doralisa de Medina, the pride and joy of the núcleo. Doralisa was Maestro Abreu's first piano teacher and holds a very special place in the history of El Sistema. This ensemble is also their students' first opportunity to come together as a full symphony orchestra complete with woodwinds, brass, and percussion sections. We worked on an arrangement of Benjamin Britten's *Young Person's Guide to the Orchestra*. Our orchestra's timpanist, a brand new musician to the núcleo who could hardly reach his instrument, was supported by a *tallerista* (an itinerant teaching-artist) playing side-by-side, a common occurrence in El Sistema. During our rehearsal, we emphasized *listening* to realize our instrumental voices as *interdependent*, yet in agreement. "How are the flutes articulating the melody? Can we match your phrasing to fit the cellos' *legato* accompaniment? What *color* of sound can you provide?" I asked the flute players.

That an orchestra and its members should recognize themselves as interdependent is an interesting notion. The term, embraced by Maestro Abreu, stems from the field of economics. The orchestra becomes, "a whole of which the parts are connected and react on each other," borrowing from the words of the nineteenth century mathematician Antoine Cournot, who wrote about economic interdependence. Beauty is realized in *equilibrium* with others. "An orchestra is a community that comes together with the fundamental objective of agreeing with itself, therefore, those who play a part in the orchestra begin to live the *experience* of agreement," the maestro explains.

Making artistic decisions as a community and while being *aware* of the interdependent contributions of others is a way to begin thinking of the orchestra as a model for social engagement or as "a new school of social life."

Through orchestral practice, participants may also come to envision their music-making as an opportunity to ascertain the value of their own voices well beyond the threads of musical interaction. Reflecting on this same idea, a fellow Venezuelan conductor pointed out, "Young musicians. . . they have to think about which instruments are playing: the strings, the woodwinds, and percussion. This challenges our students' intellect and allows them to broaden their own view of and their role in life." That very same sense of conscientious awareness allows students to *practice* coming to terms with the norms of shared consensus. A "new school of social life" also means that people can come to learn to agree, in spite of their own differences.

THE LANGUAGE OF THE INVISIBLE

"What is it that the orchestra has planted in the souls of its members? A sense of harmony, a sense of order implicit in the rhythm, a sense of the aesthetic, the beautiful and the universal, and the language of the invisible, of the invisible transmitted unseen through music."

–José Antonio Abreu

I asked a student what made the Venezuelan orchestras play with such inspiration. "They have charisma," he said. "Everyone brings their own self into the music, and every musician looks for new things that they can bring. Any average orchestra can play Arturo Marquez's *Danzón No. 2,* but we make it special, because we don't just focus on the notes, we focus on *being* the music."

Sir Simon Rattle, the world-renowned conductor, has also expressed that "music is always about something— it is not just itself. Part of the reason we feel these profound emotions from the Venezuelan musicians is that clearly the music, at its core, means the world to them, hence its messages become loud and clear."

In order to embrace artistry to its fullest potential, a musician must always feel a personal connection to the music, thus creating new meaning and experiences. As Gustav Mahler himself would explain, "It should be one's sole endeavor to see everything afresh and create it anew." When we adopt this premise, we can feel music as a living entity; flexible and malleable to the spirit of the times.

It is evident that part of El Sistema's artistic success stems from their students' desire to be truly engaged with the music that they play. The narratives inherent in music literally *move* the orchestras. The powerful "experience constants" embedded in the great Classical and Romantic masterworks guide their potent music-making. For that same reason, their repertoire is very carefully chosen.

They'll often play Beethoven's epic *Fifth Symphony*. It is a narrative of self-determination and very much in tune with their aspirations. The revolutionary score takes us from the minor to the major, from darkness to light—illuminating a passionate narrative that ultimately re-solves in triumph. This is something that any young musi-cian can identify with. It is a *universal* message. (The *Fifth* knows no geographical boundaries. In playing Beethoven, young people from the *barrios* of Caracas, the *favelas* in Bahía, or the neighborhoods of West Baltimore can all come to embrace and embody the same narrative as their own.)

It is in the observance of the universal that students come to discern a space for developing a holistic self, a fitting place from which they can lead healthy lives. The Venezuelans often elaborate on the notion of harmonizing the self through music as one of El Sistema's most salient priorities. "We are not developing musicians necessarily, we are developing human beings," says Bolivia Bottome, FundaMusical Bolívar's elegant director of institutional development.

In his book, *Meaning and Emotion in Music*, Leonard Meyer considered that the ability of a group or individual to associate a universal symbolic meaning from music's content and narrative (melody, harmony, rhythm, or lyrics) touches upon the fabric of how individual listeners may relate to one another. This is the language of the invisible at work. The goodness that is *transmitted unseen through music*, the kind of music-making that Maestro Abreu has envisioned for the members of his orchestras. A feeling of empathy made manifest in the corporeal and the spiritual. For beauty and goodness are indivisible.

Because musicians in El Sistema can grow up together and make music throughout their entire youth, it allows them to recognize themselves as ever-evolving purveyors of the many messages of music. In El Sistema, we hear a powerful sound because artistry encompasses an entire dimension of uniquely personal and collective aspirations, reflected in and through the music that they play. When Gustavo Dudamel conducts, he also feels music as part of something much deeper, a "big soul," he says. "You see the faces, the eyes, the smiles. They [the children] need music. When we are playing, we are giving all of our energy, like it is the last time, or the first time." This feeling of artistic deliverance can only help musicians transcend both as individuals and as a community, extending the possibilities of music far beyond the notes, and into new realms of human expression and achievement.

Clearly, the musicians of El Sistema have found a way to unlock the often guarded powers of *high art* and bring them to a level playing field. Upon reflective observation, I am compelled to hypothesize that theirs is an art that they *feel* to be neither at their service nor beyond their realm of inventive influence. The healthy tension that inhabits in this space of artistic compromise ignites potent sparks of creativity that leads students to feel, embrace, and grasp classical music in ways that very few have come to envision. And with the notion of community being right at the center of it all, it spouts forth reasons to equate the experience of *interpreting* art as an entry point into a realm of beauty and collective empathy. The deep and mysterious language of art—a purveyor of the aesthetic and the good—is a generous vehicle to conquer the *freedoms* that may lead us to become more hopeful human beings.

THE SPIRIT OF MUSIC

Santa Rosa is a picturesque colonial town just outside of Barquisimeto. It is also the home to *La Divina Pastora*, Venezuela's most revered patron saint. Just over two years ago, a núcleo was started there. Most lessons take place outside and in buildings around the main square—in homes, a *jefatura* (mayor's office), and parochial class-rooms. Music is heard in and around every corner of the square. José Luis Giménez (the son of Maestro Luis Giménez) is the núcleo's decisive founder. He is building a remarkable program.

"We don't always have all of the resources. Sometimes a bit of shade is all you will need for music to flourish," says Giménez, as he points to a cello teacher leading a lesson underneath a small tree. As we walk around the open-air núcleo, I hear students practicing away, and *painting* a landscape of sounds, as in Montalbán. Although this time around, the juxtaposition of indiscriminate pitches makes it sound more like *chance* music (or something

John Cage would have composed). It is very hot and humid outside, but no one seems to mind.

Giménez proudly tells me that almost five hundred students are now enrolled. "We have two orchestras playing arrangements of Dvorak's *Ninth Symphony*, a large children's choir, and a recently formed cello ensemble." He wants the entire community to be involved and is actively recruiting as many youngsters he can find. "If I can get *all* of our kids to participate, then we will be on the right path," he says.

Immediately, I think of Maestro Abreu. "Art implies a sense of perfection, therefore of excellence—a *path* to excellence," he always says.

"We want to bring everyone in this path, but there may be no more room. We are imploring the Virgin that we may have an adequate space for teaching. I know it will come," the faithful leader says. Plans to build an official rehearsal space are underway. A dedicated parent, who is also an architect, has donated her services to render a model and blueprint. It will be a modest space that will overlook the lush Turbia Valley and the verdant hills around Barquisimeto—music nestled amid a pastoral setting. Beethoven would have loved this place.

"Things start slowly. They take time," a teacher says.

The hopeful youngsters at Santa Rosa rehearse daily. They don't want to waste any time as they strive towards producing a debut concert at *La Sede* in Caracas. They *want* to be heard. Their energy is contagious; their sound is enormous. The orchestra is a serious commitment for both the students and their families. Not a single child missed a rehearsal during my time there. Everyone brought an incredible focus to their playing.

Giménez also won't rest. He wants every youngster in his community to be involved, and he means it.

Even as we are driving towards the main square to attend our rehearsals, he is quick to notice, walking away from the square, a forlorn teenager who appears to be *lost*. He stops the car, rolls down the window, and asks him, "Why aren't you in the núcleo? It's after school. It's not your place to wander around the streets.

"It's dangerous. Head the other way. I'll get you an instrument to play!"

To see how an entire town is literally being summoned to music is indeed very special. A strong leader is framing the arts as a conduit for social development of the highest order. The orchestra is now being seen as an asset and as a vehicle to elevate the town's quality of life. The main square is now a hub for music. It has also become a place of peace; and blessed by the gracious spirit of *La Divina Pastora*, who watches over the orchestra and all those who play a part in it. *"Wherever there is music, there is also hope,"* they say.

A RELENTLESS WORK ETHIC

El Sistema orchestras in Venezuela excel in many ways, yet one of their most remarkable assets is their relentless *work ethic*. In his luminous essay, *El Sistema's Open Secrets*, Eric Booth, a scholar of teaching artistry, refers to the "intensity and focus of musical study" as a foremost El Sistema ideal. Prior to my visit in Venezuela, Eric kindly shared the idea of examining the "force and durability of the motivation" behind the young musician's yearning to aspire. Where does the burning desire to blossom into beauty and virtuosity stem from? Is this something that can be taught? What can we learn?

I was invited to work with the Orquesta Sinfónica Juvenil Franco Medina on Tchaikovsky's *Fifth Symphony*. It was a four-hour rehearsal. After we had gotten to know each other, I asked when it would be appropriate to have a short break. They all said, "We don't need a break. Let's keep going!" (For a conductor who is also used to following union rules in professional orchestra settings, this had me a bit baffled. No break, well that's new, I thought.)

The *Franco Medina* orchestra is composed of musicians between the ages of thirteen and fifteen. They have come out of El Sistema Lara's systematic approach to scaffold orchestral instruction (this is the second most advanced orchestra in the program's curriculum). Their ability to embrace musical goals with utmost diligence and curiosity is part of what makes their sound come alive so readily. It is also how they advance so quickly—from arrangements of Tchaikovsky's *Marche Slave* to unabridged Mahler Symphonies, in just a few years' time. The system has produced a long lineage of best practices and tools for talent development.

But how do they learn so quickly? Learning is happening at a dramatic pace, in part, because the youngsters have many role models to look up to. The artistic prowess of El Sistema is carefully documented. Young musicians can easily stream *YouTube* videos and be inspired by the virtuosity of the Teresa Carreño Youth Orchestra (the national flagship high school age ensemble). In Barquisimeto, while playing Marquez's *Danzón No. 2*, many musicians even go as far as imitating or "borrowing" from their motions and fingerings as they go through the piece. Even during our rehearsals of Tchaikovsky's *Fifth Symphony*, it was easier to describe a bowing and articulation of sound by pointing directly to a *virtual* performance of the piece by another fellow Venezuelan orchestra, a few hundred miles away!

Aesthetics of Generosity

In the *Age of the Internet*, learning can happen in unconventional, yet very organic ways. A twelve-year-old French horn player and aspiring conductor is learning to conduct the repertoire of his own children's orchestra by watching more experienced conductors work on the same pieces with other sister orchestras around the country. "I take the scores and conduct while the video plays, and that's how I can learn the music," he says.

Back to our orchestra rehearsal, as we continued to work on Tchaikovsky's Fifth, we centered on building a musical narrative on a variety of moods. Tempo changes had to be worked out between sections, but even more important, the connotations of such rhapsodic episodes had to be realized through a painstaking process to find the *right* sounds. Especially the clarinet opening, it is such an ominous music—dark, somber, somewhat ghostly. We tried it many times. Our lead clarinetist was more than willing to oblige.

I learned that he travels from Tamaca to Barquisimeto on a raggedy bus every day to attend his orchestra rehearsals. On a good day, it may take about two hours each way. He is also learning Shostakovich's *Tenth Symphony*. It is part of a major audition leading to his dream of playing in of one Caracas' finest youth orchestras. For him, the orchestra is the great motivator.

El Sistema operates through a system of meritocracy. Students know that if they work hard enough, they may win an audition to be placed in more advanced orchestras, or even better, take part in their Latin American Academies in Caracas—a series of workshop opportunities aimed at developing talent at the highest level possible. These workshops bring the students a wealth of new knowledge as high-profile performers and teachers spend time working with them one-on-one. Edicson Ruiz, once a student of the double-bass Academy (and now a teacher), auditioned for a place at the acclaimed Berlin Philharmonic and was chosen as its youngest member.

Success comes from allowing students the opportunity to dream big. This idea is in many ways parallel to the goal-setting theory put forward by Edwin Locke, where as a general rule: "clear, particular, and difficult goals will carry greater motivation than easy, general, and vague goals." In El Sistema, there are very clear artistic objectives in place. All orchestras often strive for virtuosic feats: a debut concert within just three months of musical instruction, a new concert program for intermediate ensembles every week, and complete Beethoven or Mahler Symphonic cycles for the most advanced orchestras. There is always a fine balance between what is challenging and realistic.

Students here are working with tenacious commitment. There are no other special ingredients to success. Hard work and a desire to aspire are the key to open up the prospect of such extraordinary artistic accomplishments.

FIVE-YEAR-OLDS AT PLAY

They play tiny violins. Their feet dangle from their chairs. In El Sistema, the oldest students in their youngest orchestras are only five years old. They are lovingly called the *Compotas*. "Compota is a name for baby food, a homemade fruit mix prepared for the youngest ones in Venezuela," the program's director explained. I asked Yajaira Echeverría if I could see her program in action. She kindly invited me to work with her team in Barquisimeto.

As they prepare to begin a lesson, the small children (all sporting bright fluorescent T-shirts) will assemble in a hallway and engage in what appears to be a carefully choreographed ritual. The budding musicians will march to their classroom single-file together, holding their instruments, and singing in unison. It is an impressive display. Teachers know that they must pay special attention to classroom management and this is a first step in setting up a culture of focus, discipline, and respect.

In this sense, Maestro Abreu recalled his early experience as an educator: "I was actually more focused on building discipline than on making music." To him the orchestra would serve as an *instrument* to build the foundation of a child's holistic development. To this day, he stresses his program's social focus. "There may be other artistic programs, but this is a social development program through music . . . everything that happened then and continues to happen now is a direct consequence from this concept," he explains.

The *Compotas* are taught to think and feel like an orchestra from the get-go. They are seated in orchestral formation and are led by a conductor. The experience is not just about learning to play an instrument well, but also nurturing a culture of collaboration: sitting with stand partners, playing together, and following the instructions of a conductor. Yajaira, who is leading from a portable keyboard, isn't the only teacher in the room. Six other adult monitors help teach the orchestra. Every teacher is seated with their corresponding orchestral section. There are small enough instruments for everyone. Toy-looking trumpets and timpani sets come in bright colors!

Their conductor, a young student in training, calls the group to attention. "*Atención!*"

"*Sí, Señor!*" the students respond in unison. It is a loud response. Their energy is quickly harnessed and directed to the music.

"Let's begin, and remember we have a guest. How do we behave when we have visitors?" she asks. All of a sudden the stakes are higher. I sense the room becoming quieter and more focused. The children know they are about to perform—they've entered performance mode. As Yajaira begins playing an introductory tune, she also provides an unresolved progression of chords (I-IV-V) to cue the children into their performance.

They are playing one of their favorite songs, *The Grillito* or "The Cricket." The piece is part of a collection especially composed for the group. They get to play, sing, and engage their whole body in rhythmic exercises. It is an ingenious little piece of music. It encompasses simple melodies with open strings and the use of their first finger only. By limiting the difficulty, the teachers can direct the students' focus on their bow hold, left hand position, and placement of their instrument: crucial building blocks for beginner string players.

There are even a few effects written in, a cricket's squeak and shriek is aptly rendered through extended bowing techniques. Bowing behind the bridge to produce a *scratch tone* is a device to turn imagery into sound. These extended techniques, which are usually reserved for very advanced players and featured in some of the most demanding string repertoire, like that of Krzysztof Penderecki and Béla Bartók, become a natural extension of their classroom experience. And proof that in El Sistema nothing comes too early.

"Our program is more like an experiment, a way for teachers to discover new teaching techniques and help prepare our children to advance quickly into the next line of orchestras," Yahaira explains. "They can begin at two years old. It is never too soon to start!" she says. Although different forms of early childhood musical immersion exist within El Sistema, the *Compota* program (to my knowledge) is not part of the system's national plan, but its leaders in Barquisimeto hope that it can expand to other núcleos around the state.

The value of early childhood education cannot be underestimated. These programs can be most beneficial in terms of creating a long lasting impact in the lives of young people. Current research in education and specifically that related to early childhood education is already pointing us in that direction. The Harvard Center for the Developing Child has uncovered critical connections between early childhood interventions and the development of executive functioning skills. The strengthening of these important life skills: inhibitory control, working memory, and mental flexibility, as explained in the paper, *Building the Brain's "Air Traffic Control" System: How Early Experiences Shape the Development of Executive Function*, are proven to be strong links between early school achievement and a student's social, emotional, and moral development. Interestingly enough, children between the ages of three and five are the most susceptible for gains in the development of these skills, making the *Compota* program or any other related early childhood musical intervention prone to be increasingly successful in the long run.

Although attempting to tie the development of executive functioning skills to purported outcomes of music education is a promising idea, it must be further explored and probed through specific research design frameworks before it can be incorporated into public policy recommendations. Many scholars, practitioners, and other thinkers are already exploring this possibility. In the interim, I shall provide a few preliminary observations (from an artistic lens) as to how the orchestra may enhance the development of these important skills.

Ensemble-based rehearsals would require *inhibitory control* to build discipline and empathy, *working memory* to hold and manipulate musical instructions over a period of time, and *mental flexibility* to "adjust to changing demands, priorities, and perspectives." In the *Compota* program, students work on perfecting their playing and ascertaining their role in the ensemble, thus strengthening their ability to filter distractions and control impulses. As they begin working on repertoire and playing by rote, they learn to hold and manipulate information over time. Throughout the learning process, their teachers will also give them constant feedback, fostering a lively space of exchange where students participate and acquire new knowledge and skills.

As a multi-dimensional intervention for children in a variety of settings and circumstances, music education, because it develops both cognitive and emotional capacities, has the potential to "shape positive behaviors and improve levels of mental acuity" altogether. Replicating programs like *Compota* can lead us to continue to propose the arts as a valuable component of educational curricula. The Harvard research supports the claim, noting that focusing our attention on the development of *executive functioning* in students beyond literacy education can be beneficial for the evolution of education in our times.

MOVING ALONG

As the ten Fellows traveled together across the country, we would always find time to reflect upon the work we had experienced, the friends we had made, or the music we had played together. Often times, we would also exchange thoughts and ideas on how teachers and leaders in El Sistema have been able to articulate such profound pedagogical and organizational paradigm shifts in benefit of their students. And specially, how often they give so much of themselves in spite of any difficulties that may come their way. Ultimately, they know that their work *matters*, but it also takes a strong vision and determination to reach "the pinnacle of the hill."

Traveling again also meant that we would continue a hopeful journey and *struggle* into the unknown, exploring new trails and meaningful opportunities for growth. My colleague Julie Davis, a violinist from Syracuse, told a deeply moving (and metaphorical) story that expressed this same feeling:

"I came to understand the magic of El Sistema while traveling in a twelve-passenger van with a broken air conditioner amidst the rural Venezuelan state of Guárico. Too restless to sleep but too tired to read, I spent the majority of the six-hour ride watching the bumpy dirt road roll out in front of my view, reflecting upon the experience that the foreign country had offered me so far.

"Our van continued moving along the dirt road when a giant hill suddenly appeared in our path. I laughed to myself considering the chances that the van, loaded with ten other passengers and their luggage, would manage to make it up the small mountain. Avoiding mounds of dirt and evading large potholes, I breathed a sigh of relief as we fought to reach the pinnacle of the hill.

"We had made it!

"And then we began the descent, and I realized the struggle wasn't over.

"We had to dodge a plethora of potholes on the other side of the hill as well. And to me, that's what El Sistema embodies—a relentless struggle to better the lives of thousands through music, knowing every day's successes will bring more challenges to overcome."

To feel that your learning has just begun (all of the time) is part of an educator's formula for success. I know this same feeling is also part of a life in music. How many times does one *finish* studying a piece of music, only to realize that there is so much more to explore?

Finding Purpose

At Valle de la Pascua, a small rural town in the heart of Venezuela's state of Guárico, Tchaikovsky's *Romeo and Juliet Overture* never sounded so endearing to me. It is a score undeniably compelling—the heart-rending story of two star-crossed lovers—one that we know almost too well. In our rehearsal, I asked the students to imagine themselves in the story of the music and give in to the drama of the Shakespearian narrative. Without hesitation the musicians quickly became absorbed by the music. It was an electrifying exchange. It was so intense that during our rehearsal the power went out. Somehow the orchestra didn't miss a beat! For an instant (which seemed like an eternity) we continued in darkness; finding our way back to a dimly lit room and striving to uncover a sense of ownership and purpose to *our* music-making.

El Sistema in Venezuela has fashioned persuasive paradigms for the rationale and purpose of art. Music is never seen as a luxury, but as a natural extension of a young person's life. In Mahomito, at a very poor elementary school, we heard a group of choristers singing a repertoire of *boleros*, *merengues*, and *música llanera* (songs from the Venezuelan plains).

I saw young children holding hands, feeling every nuance in the songs, and cherishing the splendor of doing something well together. Many of them were immersed in the musical experience, eyes closed, as if somehow they had found their own *sanctuary* of peace. They were proud to perform for us.

Very seldom have I experienced such potent musicianship. In their performance, I heard a new kind of intention and aesthetic of sound. Their music in two-part harmony accompanied by the energetic strumming of a *cuatro* shone with palpable relevance—illuminating the crowded rehearsal room and bringing many of us to tears. What made their performance so moving?

I couldn't help but think of the children's own life stories and musical aspirations. Why do they sing? Why does it matter so much? It became clear to me that the children of El Sistema sing and play because it brings them to a world of tangible opportunity, giving them a new sense of unencumbered freedom that allows them to express themselves.

Music serves as an instrument for social transformation in that it adds concrete value to their lives, providing for the opening of new perspectives amid the challenges that they may encounter where they reside (where more often than not, the living conditions are precarious on many levels). In a space where opportunities are scarce, music is the conduit for *striving* for a better life, because it allows its participants to find the paths to aliveness and resilience, or in the words of the Christian mystic Meister Eckhart, to uncover the "hope of loving or being loved."

Building a harmonious spirit is a way to overcome the tensions of material poverty. And this is why every note might be purposefully and intentionally defined with a new identity, colored with a sense of urgency and care at the same time. In an orchestra or a choir, participants blossom through the sharing of profound artistic experiences and the rendering of beauty through collaboration (a theme that has been consistent throughout my immersion into El Sistema in Venezuela).

Most students I've spoken to have told me that "music is their life," or that "it brings them to a place of possibility." Both statements echo the words of Maestro Abreu as he instructs fellow educators on the role of *artistic doingness*: "Let us reveal to our children the beauty of music and music shall reveal to them the beauty of life."

In pursuing music, students generate a level of motivation that leads to re-imagining a new purpose in life, creating both improved social environments and poignant music-making experiences. This framework gives us a new aesthetic of possibility where students' capacity for growth is extended as far as the universe of music. It is only up to each individual to decide how far they may choose to go.

FOR MUSIC, FOR COUNTRY

"When one creates a new orchestra, one also creates a new world—a meeting point of dialogue and harmony for our youngsters. I see every orchestra as if it were Venezuela. Our country is present in every one of them."

–José Antonio Abreu

Ask any taxi driver in Calabozo to take you to *la orquesta* and he will usher you straight to the right place (no address needed). It would seem that almost everyone, in large and small towns alike, knows where music is taking place. "Thank you for teaching our youngsters," I've heard. I quickly tell my driver that most of the time it's the other way around—they are teaching me.

In Venezuela, orchestras and choirs often manifest themselves as emblems of national identity. During a rehearsal with the children's orchestra at the Antonio Estévez Núcleo (named after the composer of *Cantata Criolla*) we set out to conquer their first reading of *Venezuela*.

Scored for an intermediate level symphony orchestra, it is in many ways the equivalent of a national anthem. It has that kind of singular resonance to it. The melody is strikingly emotive.

Delving into our work, I thanked the children for allowing me to lead them in such a special piece. As we began solving some of the technical issues inherent in the score, we paid attention to *balancing* the voices. "Let us hear the woodwinds soar above the strings. The trumpets need a more rounded sound," I requested. Equally important here was to inquire what other associations may derive from playing this music, and for what end?

"It is a piece from my homeland, Venezuela!" a young double-bassist shouted with a decisive flair. "The piece should reflect a feeling of joy, and pride, and also love," the students remarked. The children agreed that it should reflect aspects of their own lives. "Do you have any similar pieces from your own country?" they asked in return.

"The works of Carlos Chávez and José Pablo Moncayo reflect the musical heritage of Mexico, the country I grew up in," I said. My colleague Julie Davis, sitting in the viola section and team teaching with me (a signature El Sistema practice) played us an excerpt of *America the Beautiful*, a melody from her homeland. The children listened attentively focusing on every note—a sign of their ability to play ambassadors.

These kinds of inquiry-based learning experiences should always be part of a music educator's pedagogical thinking. John Dewey, the educational reformer, theorized on the value of this practice. Education should begin with curiosity and follow "a spiral path of inquiry where students are asking, investigating, reflecting, and discussing." It is the teacher's role to be a guide in this process of self-discovery.

Because pieces like *Venezuela*, *Cielito Lindo* (traditional from Mexico), or *America the Beautiful* may bring forth feelings of unity and are a source of national pride, they ought to be played often. Renditions of *Venezuela* are heard everywhere here: in orchestral and choral settings, and even as recorder flute arrangements. *They are meant to be played for a lifetime.*

Creating a culture of participants in the arts requires us to turn to national culture as a source of inspiration. To the extent that students connect with their heritage, music can be an effective tool to usher in ideals for the shaping of engaged and devoted citizens.

At the end of our rehearsal today *Venezuela* sounded beautifully. The children chanted, *"Sí se pudo"* (yes we could). They were proud to have conquered the music for themselves, and for their country.

MUSIC SHALL FLOW

Deep in the heart of Guárico, I came across a folk music ensemble made up of a combination of traditional acoustic and modern electric instruments. As they played a set of *joropos* (a musical style resembling the waltz), I directed my attention to a young percussionist in the group. His playing had an unusual strength—an uncanny intensity and focus. He was featured as a soloist in many of the pieces that the group played for us. He had a serious look on his face. Every time he played, he appeared to have been *lost* in the moment and in the music. Yet he was always in control of his playing; improvising complex rhythmic accompaniments with his set of maracas, every so often becoming enraptured in moments of virtuosity, and narrowing his focus with each passing measure.

For an artist, these are exactly the kind of events that transpire during what we may describe as an "inspired" performance. This quality of engagement may signal that a performer has made the journey from musician to artist, entering into that mysterious yet very desirable place of ultimate creative prowess.

It is a phenomenal effect. I've seen it all throughout Venezuela while hearing individual musicians and even entire ensembles. Is it replicable? Where might this fountain of artistic prowess stem from? Many scholars have studied the psychology behind these acts of virtuosity. The positive psychologist Mihaly Csikszentmihalyi (pronounced "CHEEK-sent-mə-HY-ee") calls this same effect optimal performance or *flow*. While attaining flow or "being in the zone," a musician's field of attention becomes focused, one's subjective experience of time is altered, thus creating a state of mind that lives in joy and possibility, he explains. In his book, *Optimal Experience: Psychological Studies of Flow in Consciousness*, he contends that in order to achieve a state of flow, there must be "a balance between the challenges perceived and the skills a person brings to it." In that sense, the educator must be able to find where those intersections meet and assign repertoire accordingly.

If we are to provide "optimal" opportunities for students to thrive and express their sensibilities, we should assign repertoire that is not too easy yet difficult enough to procure a decent challenge. Every piece, no matter its level or that of the ensemble, should sound fluid and natural. Even the most novice ensembles should aim to produce performances of a professional caliber.

Fostering a balance between challenge and skill allows fresh motivation to emerge, which helps students remain occupied and interested in their own musical development. This need not apply only to El Sistema orchestras. In effect, the same principle can be extended into the realm of arts learning as a whole.

Very often I've heard from students in núcleos that their orchestra is a place where they can forget about the stresses of everyday life. "I can forget about my worries," they say. Music takes up so much of the students' creative energies and to be successful in it, they must focus deeply in their work. As they come to immerse themselves in music, any physical entropies (the usual preoccupations of everyday life) Csikszentmihalyi contends, can be wiped away.

Flow in music is also part of connecting with the invisible in art. As a musician, I've also come to experience its effects. And anytime this happens, whether it is in a rehearsal or a performance, it is yet another reason to celebrate the gift of music.

LETTING THEM PLAY

Much has been said about peer-learning as a foremost El Sistema pedagogical ideal. How do these collaborations manifest in the life of a núcleo? Where does a student's desire to participate and contribute to the learning experiences of others stem from?

In Barquisimeto, I came across two young violinists practicing away in the núcleo's playground. They were completely immersed in their music. It was an elegant *Concerto Grosso* by Arcangelo Corelli, the Italian Baroque composer. As they got to a difficult passage on the second page, the more advanced girl would stop the other and point at her music to offer advice:

"Try it down bow. It works better."

They would begin the piece again. This time played at a much faster tempo.

"It is getting too fast. The sixteenth notes are coming!"

"It's okay. Try to play it anyways. I'll take the lead!"

These episodes (of students helping each other) can happen in very organic ways. The students here seemed to have internalized the idea that in order to grow, they must help others grow as well. Some of the most inspired moments of teaching and learning often happen outside of the classroom—amid the hallways as students wait for a lesson, in the form of impromptu performances in cafeterias, or informal jam sessions in a parking lot. By playing outside classroom walls, the prevalence (if any) of vertically directive teacher-student structures might become appropriately dissolved.

Johann Pestalozzi, the nineteenth century Swiss educational reformer, spoke of education as being most effective when it became "radically personal and appealing to each learner's intuition." I suspect the young violinists felt their own playground as *radically personal*. They had an adventurous and uniquely intuitive approach to their music-making; framed away from the confines of closed spaces or unnecessary authority.

I also caught my colleague David France teaching a violin lesson in the porch of a house. He was going through a movement of the Bruch *Violin Concerto* listening for intonation problems and correcting his young student's technique. (The boy seemed to be having trouble keeping his triplets steady and in tune.) There was much to work to do. David put a metronome on his music stand, and slowly, they began building up the tempo. "OK, play it for me at *moderato*. Now, let's speed up a little more!" There they were, working very carefully on the piece.

Then out of nowhere, a piercing beat begins to sound. It's not the metronome. The sound is coming from far away. "It's a *trenecito!*" (a makeshift trolley to parade people around town). As the trenecito approaches the house, the flamboyant music has grown much louder—it is an entrancing soundscape. It is playing *Reggaeton* (a hybrid of dancehall and electronica). The lesson continued and the student began to play the Bruch alongside the beat of the same music, as if *soloing* with it. It is an unusual pairing, but somehow this has become a memorable learning experience.

Child-centered education in music begins with educators recognizing themselves as *moderators* of a larger learning process. Imparting the right tools and then trusting children to synthesize them and perfect them through their own lens of experience must be the music teacher's goals in El Sistema and elsewhere. Students can design their own experiences, making out of informal activities, powerful opportunities to engage fully and passionately with their music, as if it were a natural part of life.

BEAUTY IS TO TRUST

EVERY REHEARSAL IS AN OPPORTUNITY TO LEARN. I asked the most advanced students in Calabozo whether they would be interested in working on a piece from the Classical repertoire. We picked a Mozart Serenade, his most popular one, the *Eine Kleine Nachtmusik*. It is not an *easy* piece. In fact, it is very difficult to play. There are many details in the score. Dynamic markings have to be meticulously observed. The composer will often place staccatos and slurs on specific notes and phrases. Cadences must be resolved with utmost care and grace. In other words, one has to learn to be an extremely disciplined musician. Students must *listen* very carefully. It is extremely taxing to play this music.

The music of Mozart is absolute. There is no program or story to describe it. Its meaning is derived from how one balances its architecture; how one is able to fashion every single note, like a pearl. "If you can learn to play Mozart well, you will be able to play anything," I told them. And then we began.

It took us a while to find the right tempo. We had to work very hard at trying to balance the weight of the inner voices. What happens when four instrumental voices are to be playing simultaneously, but only one is to be heard above the rest? Do the other voices hold back or should they support the main melody, and how?

If the music is absolute and does not symbolize any *emotions* or characters as in programmatic works like Rimsky-Korsakov's elegant *Scheherazade* or Stravinsky's lively *Petrouchka*, how do you come to tell the story? How do you establish a personal connection to the music and then transmit it to your audience? I could sense the young musicians were quite overwhelmed. It was a lot to think about. The tin-roof-covered room was dimly lit. It was getting very hot and increasingly difficult to focus.

"Let's put the music away," I said. "What is beauty?" I asked.

"Beauty is order and perfection," I heard.

"But really, what is beauty?" I asked again.

And then, I heard from the back of the first violin section one of the most interesting yet actionable descriptions of the word: "Beauty is to trust."

"Beauty is to allow for the feeling of music to take over. To let the music guide you to the unknown."
The room was silent. You could hear a pin drop.

"I think you've discovered a powerful truth in the aesthetics of orchestral playing," I said. "Let us try the Mozart again and think about what you just expressed.

"But let's try the introduction again, and this time when we get to measure 5, I'll ask the first violins to trust that you will produce a homogeneous sound, and trust that the seconds, violas, and celli, will move together in perfect rhythmic harmony and synchronicity with you. Trust that you will all feel the music together.

"In a spirit of trust, I will cue you in and then step aside—you play it on your own," I said.

It worked. A new world of sound opened up. Everyone began listening more intently. Their tempo was more stable. The music had a unique strength. It spoke more clearly. It had come from a place of trust.

The orchestra *works* when musicians come to recognize and trust in the skills of others. In this framework, the act of music-making can be seen not just as a deeply affective experience, but also as a metaphor for building social capital, the foundation for what Robert Putnam calls "civic virtue." Putnam, a notable scholar on the effects of community ties, articulates in the *Journal of Democracy* that "social capital refers to connections among individuals—social networks and the norms of reciprocity and trustworthiness that arise from them."

In an orchestra, a participant's musical responsibilities may quickly migrate into contractual ones. And those in turn can translate into a sense of moral duty that will drive instrumentalists to play their best, and therefore raise the quality of music-making across the board. "Community connectedness is never about warm fuzzy tales of civic triumph. In measurable and well-documented ways, social capital makes an enormous difference to people's lives," Putnam notes.

In order to achieve any meaningful success, the orchestra and its members will have to trust that everyone will play their part beautifully and in consonance with the others. Enacting trust will ultimately "allow citizens [and in our case musicians] to resolve collective problems more easily and to realize an awareness of the many ways in which their fates are linked."

And these *fates* may extend well beyond music. In a *Scientific American* article, Paul J. Zak, a neuroeconomist at Claremont University, discovered that trust is among the strongest known predictors of a country's wealth— nations with low levels of trust among their citizens tend to be poor. "Their inhabitants will undertake too few of the long-term investments that create jobs and raise incomes," he explains.

As noted here, people's well-being may be utterly dependent on their ability to trust in themselves and in others. Seeking a "harmonic interdependence of voices and instruments," as Maestro Abreu instructs us, requires musicians to enact a sublime sense of trust. The same experience can guide them to build social capital, foster relationships, and begin to see the world through a lens of mutually beneficial connectedness. The orchestra may not be just about the music, but also about other profound truths that may be inextricably linked to discovering new opportunities for both social and moral growth.

AUTHENTICITY

Discerning beauty in art has to be part of a thoughtful process of reflection and connection with the work of art itself and in the context of a multi-dimensional realm of experience. In her essay, *Curriculum and Consciousness*, Maxine Greene explored engaging with literature to uncover new realms of meaning. Drawing from the teachings of Jean-Paul Sartre, she explained that in order to come to terms with a work of art, a participant must seek to recreate it in terms of his own consciousness. In order to "penetrate it, to experience it existentially and empathetically," he must try to place himself within what Maurice Blanchot called the *interior space.*

A high-school-age cellist asked to speak to me after orchestra rehearsal. We had been playing Tchaikovsky's *Serenade for Strings* together. "Maestro, I would like to play something for you," she said. It was past nine o'clock and the núcleo was about to close. "Let us get together for a lesson tomorrow," I suggested. She gently said no. She wanted to play for me right then. I obliged.

It was noisy in the room. The orchestra musicians were packing and chatting, but as she started playing the opening movement of Bach's *First Cello Suite,* her friends gravitated towards us, and all of a sudden we had an audience. Her playing had a strong inner pulse, an agreeable tone, many of the elements of a finished performance.

"Let's work on your phrasing," I said. "What do you want to say?"

"My teacher says one should feel the music. Then the music will work."

"Yes, but that's only the beginning. How will you come to uncover the meaning of the music? Try to also bring your intellect inside the impulse of the music," I said.

She played again for us. This time she emphasized the arches of the melody.

"Be bold," I said. "Show us where the melody begins, show us where it ends." (I learned this from Sir Simon Rattle as he instructed his musicians, echoing the words of Leopold Mozart, "Every sound begins and ends in silence.")

"Now, play it with more freedom."

"What does that mean?" she asked.

"It means that you must always be in control of the shapes of the phrases."

"Should it be more improvisatory?"

"Yes, absolutely," I agreed. "Now, let me suggest that you try playing the opening theme, let's say three times, in three different ways. Make slight variations of the dynamics, play with the length and *expression* of notes, and with the weight and lightness of the sound, but make it a *conscious* effort. In other words, put yourself inside the core of the music."

She tried it three different ways.

"Now pick one, which do you like best? And remember that your choice will be the right one, because you have made a conscious artistic decision," I said.

In retrospect, I think we might also have been testing the "authenticity" of the *Cello Suite*. Howard Gardner, the esteemed cognitive psychologist, whom I heard speak at the Harvard Graduate School of Education a few months before, explained that any work of art may be authentic to the extent that it captures aspects of *experience* in meaningful ways. And my lesson with her was exactly that—an evocative experiment on uncovering traits of authenticity.

What was compelling about it? The music of Bach of course, *and* the novel connections she established with the music itself. She recognized the "memorability" of its form, its "interestingness," and was therefore compelled to revisit the opening page three times, in different ways. She heard the music "fresh and anew," and made performance choices while internalizing the experience of the piece as her own. Through the *process*, beauty was revealed before our eyes.

If we are to make music transcend beyond the notes, we must also strive to reveal its virtues through a personal and deeply feeling lens of "authenticity." Channeling a score through a performance that is derived from our very own experience of being in the *interior space* of it—seeing, hearing, and imagining the work in manifold and infinite varieties—will allow for inspired connections to be made between the music and its interpreter.

For our goals in fashioning art, as the Greek philosopher Aristotle would attest, should be "to represent not the outward appearance of things, but their inward significance." That is where its strengths (and ours as musicians) may truly reside.

OUR FAVORITES

In between rehearsals, I was asked to name and describe my favorite classical works. It was a difficult question to try to answer. There are works that I certainly enjoy studying or hearing again and again, but I don't think they are necessarily *better* than others. In classical music, there are hundreds of pieces available to performers. There are the familiar *warhorses* in the repertoire: the Beethoven Symphonies and the Mozart Overtures. The Tchaikovsky Symphonies or the Vivaldi *Four Seasons*. Too many to pick and choose from!

When I think of my favorite works, I have to reflect upon their "memorability." What impact have these made on me as a student and performer of music, or as a human being? Every so often, these favorites are so because they are tied to endearing experiences. I told a group of students this personal story of growing up with a treasured piece of music:

"I was about seven years old when I first heard Mussorgsky's *Pictures at an Exhibition*. I had come into a CD store (compact discs were in fashion at the time) and unassumingly picked up my very first classical recording. I didn't know anything about the piece or the composer, but I was drawn to the picture on the cover: a mysterious, yet inviting gate. I was hooked and then I listened. It was easy to imagine pictures to the music.

"*Pictures at an Exhibition* was the only piece of music I listened to for months! I was continually drawn to the music's primal beauty—the shimmering sounds, the ominous sounds, the consonant and dissonant sounds.

"It wasn't until much later that I learned that Mussorgsky had composed the piece inspired by a series of watercolors and drawings from the memorial exhibition of a dear friend; that the movements or musical events depict an imaginary gallery tour, or that it was the French composer Maurice Ravel who had orchestrated the original piano version.

"To this day, it is still one of my favorite pieces of music. It doesn't matter how many times I've listened to it. I always seem to find new things every time: more details, nuances, *and* surprises all embedded in the depths of the miraculous orchestration.

"Have you had a similar experience? Can we ever stop learning from what a great piece of music can inspire? Do you have any *favorite* pieces of music?" I asked.

I have come to believe that any work of art is as powerful as its ability to give us reasons to come back to it. The power of a *good* work of art lies in its strength to push us to reflect on what it could mean in the context of our own lives and its force to encourage new thoughts and experiences. I often come back to the score of the Mussorgsky. I play it on the piano, conduct it with orchestras, and listen to other wide-ranging interpretations by my colleagues. On a more personal note, coming back to it also means reconnecting with unencumbered emotions if you will, fishing a memory or two from those first listening experiences during my youth.

Many of us have our favorites, and mine might be different from yours, because each of our experiences will be unique when living with them. And that is what makes the arts a crucial instrument for recognizing that everyone, regardless of position or creed, is entitled to an opinion. Classical music, as complex as it may sound to be, is that simple. It is that democratic. These experiences can be within everyone's reach.

A SACRED CALLING

Las Panelas is one of Coro's most perilous areas of town. We are told there is an implicit curfew: no one is to roam the streets alone after six o'clock. José Maiolino, El Sistema's senior leader for the state of Falcón, has invited us to visit a brand new núcleo there.

It is based out of a humble home. It is an unassuming space re-imagined for music. Isandra Campos, the núcleo's founder, is no stranger to El Sistema. Her son Ismel is a violist and member of the Simón Bolívar String Quartet, the national program's first professional string quartet, now a major act represented worldwide by *Askonas Holt* (a leading arts management agency).

As soon as the Fellows arrived at the núcleo, a group of about thirty young musicians greeted us with a *German Dance*. It was such a thoughtful gesture. At year one, their sound is characteristically El Sistema. The string players are following on a "tradition of playing" stemming all the way to Maestro Abreu's own original concept of sound, I am told. This orchestra is perhaps the closest thing to a beginner version of the Simón Bolívar Symphony Orchestra of Venezuela. They too have developed a keen sense of ownership and pride in their playing.

Gerardo Reyes, the conductor at Núcleo Las Panelas, is one of many young professionals across the country that are key in helping to sustain, develop, and expand the work of El Sistema. A music director and conductor, he is also part teacher and part social worker. It is not an easy job, and yet amid dire working conditions, he leads with decisive vision. "We will soon be playing the Telemann *Viola Concerto* with our own in-house violist. In less than three years we shall do Beethoven's Fifth," he says.

The children play, literally, by heart. Some of them have made makeshift music stands out of clothing hangers, but this is by no means a deterrent for learning. On the contrary, it is another reason not to give up on the dream of playing well together. *Music is always about joy.* That same feeling is never dependent upon having enough material resources, but based upon the idea that through music an entire orchestral community may see itself blossom anew.

Gerardo knows that his children come from the poorest strata of society. Many of them have never met their own parents. Most eat only one meal a day. Because he is deeply committed to a mission of social rescue through music, there are no limits to what he can produce with the youngsters.

"El Sistema is an engine for societal change," says my colleague Teresa Hernández, a trainer of conductors as artists and social changers for the national movement. "A children's orchestra conductor must not only conduct the music, but actively construct and model new paths of success for musicians. She must also listen carefully to correct their intonation and rhythm; making her students feel proud of themselves and their accomplishments."

Conductors are an important part of the "engine" of El Sistema. They often lead the pedagogical planning and act as fervent advocates for artistic excellence and social change. They must be at all times inside and outside the music—playing ambassadors, organizing parent meetings, raising funds, and motivating everyone to succeed. Although all of these may sound brutally daunting, the El Sistema-inspired educator should not despair of meeting such responsibilities.

As conduits between students and the orchestra, instrumental teachers are a núcleo's most valuable asset. In Venezuela, teachers learn to teach while teaching. In fact, everyone is summoned to be a teacher: from the five-year-old *Compota* students to the world-renowned *Bolívars.* Teaching and learning are fully intertwined. Out of necessity perhaps, but more likely out of a sense of responsibility for sustaining the impact and longevity of the national program.

And this is why you might have a thirteen-year-old trumpet player assisting with orchestra rehearsals, or a recent university graduate in roles that may have been originally reserved for more seasoned leaders (Sergio Teijido, one of the núcleo directors for the state of Guárico, is twenty-three years old and already in charge of directing nearly one thousand students and their teachers). To this day, Maestro Abreu, El Sistema's foremost teacher, continues to lead rehearsals to perfect his orchestras and train new conductors in Caracas. He will always place his trust in youth as a catalyst for growth.

Through an experimental approach, educators design their own curriculum leading to a student's attainment of mastery of designated orchestral repertoire. They devise their own "radically personal" systems of instruction using as many or few pedagogical tools as are available. All musical concepts (including technique, theory, and expression) are introduced through group instruction.

It has been said that "any teacher who has stopped learning has probably also stopped being useful as a teacher." It is for the same reason that teachers in El Sistema and elsewhere must always be passionate about evolving in their work, guiding students to solve problems, and posing questions that will open up new realms of thinking and habits of mind.

To the extent that teachers focus on developing their students' potential, they also will grow; and come to see their success be made manifest through the accomplishments of the students they hold dear. For teaching, and teaching alone, is a calling into the sacred empire of generosity.

Servant Leadership

"He who encourages an ideal must be capable, necessarily, to consecrate its existence to fulfillment. And for that, he must be willing to descend to the smallest and most seemingly ordinary echelons of action."

–José Antonio Abreu

Everywhere I went, I saw students and teachers willing to share their gifts and talents with others. These acts of solidarity were made manifest in many different ways.

In Coro, and tucked in a quiet corner of a courtyard, I found a group of very young instrumentalists playing recorders. They were being led by a charismatic young girl.

I approached her and asked, "Are you their teacher?"

"Yes, they are new to the núcleo, and I am helping them learn their music," she replied. "They have a very important concert coming up!"

I managed to pass along to her some ideas for leading ensembles, and she quickly absorbed many of the concepts. She asked to see my scores and was bewildered to notice so many of my own markings written in. "That's how I can learn and memorize when the woodwinds or the timpani come in. You must cue everyone in on time," I said. She then began her rehearsal again, counting off and cuing everyone with confident aplomb, "Three-and-play!" At ten years of age, she is a natural leader. It was a joy to see her teach and give so much of her budding talent to her own peers.

In Valle de la Pascua, I saw a seventeen-year-old percussionist lead a performance of some Caribbean-influenced *merengues* played with paramount joy. His musicians were eight children with special needs. Some had muscular atrophies, others were blind. But Christian never made any special distinctions or concessions. He demanded an extraordinary level of discipline and excellence from them. In the belief that out of musical excellence stems social transformation, Christian is using his musical talents to *conduct* lives. El Sistema has propelled him to see himself responsible for the *mentoring* of some of the most vulnerable members of his núcleo.

The talented teenage concertmaster of the *Franco Medina* Orchestra spends her free afternoons in Santa Rosa working diligently with students on scales, arpeggios, and exercises to perfect their weekly repertoire of arrangements of classical masterworks. Chacín is an extraordinary musician and a role model to the children. She'll help the little ones tune their instruments, tie their shoelaces, and make them smile. She naturally embodies El Sistema's social mission to the core. And she enjoys teaching. It is an honor for advanced students to do so.

In Caracas, Najaneth Perez, a long time percussion teacher at Núcleo Sarría, knows that her students are capable of accomplishments far beyond their own imagination. And that's why she works incessantly, listening to and polishing their music-making in a dusty outside patio, amid the harsh weather and the elements, because she believes that she can make a difference. All of her students matter, "every note means something" and it "adds up."

During our residency in Barquisimeto, Stephanie Hsu (also a superb violist) was invited to join their top youth orchestra in a performance of Prokofiev's *Fifth Symphony*, a score she hadn't played before. I ran into her that day and found her a bit worried about the prospect of playing the rehearsal that same evening. In her blog, she tells the story of Johander, a nineteen-year-old violist in the orchestra who offered help. Stephanie described his willingness to spend an hour coaching her through the entire piece; paying attention to the most difficult sections, looking at fingerings, bowings, and other markings. All in a genuine effort to make her feel welcomed. "I had an ally," she wrote. "Someone who was looking out for me as a member of his section . . . and he easily introduced me to all of the other violists who were equally as warm."

These are the quiet and often unrecognized acts of kindness that are very much part of the aesthetics of El Sistema.

GUSTAVO THE GREAT

Luis Giménez, Gustavo Dudamel's first violin teacher, re-called the time when his student took up the baton for the first time. "I had been late for my rehearsal with the Amadeus Children's Orchestra, and as I entered the build-ing, I heard an orchestra playing some very familiar piec-es. The rehearsal had started. It was *little* Gustavo conducting!"

The orchestra wouldn't waste any time. The music had to go on. "Conducting was like child's play for him. It was so perfectly natural." He would later go on to lead the Lara State Children's Orchestra, a huge ensemble of 800 musicians, for a city-wide festival. "Maestro Abreu was there that evening, sitting in the front row, observ-ing intently, scrutinizing every gesture and sound. It was clear from that moment on that Gustavo would go on to accomplish great things," Giménez told me. A new artis-tic leader had been identified. With the approval of his grandmother, Gustavo moved to Caracas to continue his musical studies. At seventeen years old and guided by

Maestro Abreu, his beloved mentor, he learned Mahler's *First Symphony*. The same piece that eleven years later would be the centerpiece of his inaugural concert as music director of the Los Angeles Philharmonic.

It is fascinating to see Dudamel at work. He is the kind of conductor who can move effortlessly from conducting the Berlin Philharmonic Orchestra to the Big Noise Children's Orchestra in Raploch; from the *Alma Llanera* Folk Ensemble in his native Venezuela to conducting operas at *La Scala* in Milan. I have seen him work in a variety of settings. Many critics, personalities, and fans have tried to describe him, often eliciting some peculiar adjectives and nicknames: The *Dude*, *Rockstar*, the *Elvis of the Orchestra World*. The truth of the matter is that Dudamel does not have time to be any of those. He is in fact, opposed to the idea. But it doesn't mean he won't flirt with it.

He'll often program Stravinsky's *Rite of Spring*, the same piece that back in 1913 elicited a tantrum with concertgoers in Paris, who deemed it too violent and too *avant-garde*, causing the twentieth-century audience to degenerate into a riot. He sometimes plays his violin. If you are lucky, you might hear him play *El Choclo*, a sultry Argentinean tango. A globe-trotting conductor, Dudamel has an excruciating concert schedule. He will often program new works that require lots of effort to learn and assimilate. It is part of keeping classical music alive.

Engaging with a younger generation of concertgoers seems to be very much a part of his artistic mission. He was recently heard conducting a *Concerto for Electric Cello and Orchestra* by young Mexican composer Enrico Chapela. The concerto, being something of heavy metal revelation (infusing classical forms with jazz and rock elements), features a soloist equipped with a Yamaha *e-cello* plugged to a guitar amplifier and a Roland synthesizer distorting sounds with delay effects, reverbs, and other multi-effects.

To be constantly performing means that he must be constantly rehearsing. That is where the magic of conducting really happens. It's the moment when a conductor *becomes* an educator. The conductor is to moderate an experience for his musicians, and facilitate a space where the orchestra may find its own voice through the mysterious yet deeply satisfying language of music. Music can't ever be static. It must be in constant flux and in dialogue with its beholder. Conductors must be at all times, inside and outside the music, offering insight and *listening* acutely and intently.

Although it may be difficult to pinpoint exactly what makes Dudamel a conductor that many musicians in professional orchestras love and often praise, one could say that it is his spirit of teaching with an openness of heart that elicits such favorable reviews. He teaches often and well.

I saw him rehearse Mahler's *Symphony of a Thousand* at the Shrine Auditorium in downtown Los Angeles. With over a thousand musicians on stage, his attention would be centered on the smallest details, even extra-musical ones. "Why is the brass ensemble off-stage not standing up together? Remember that you are performing, even when you are not playing!" he says in Spanish.

The playful demeanor that works well while teaching the word *stupendous* as part of a Sesame Street episode alongside Elmo, also comes in useful at the Gothenburg Symphony, where he demonstrates, by enacting a medieval scene where a gentleman bows and a lady curtsies, how cadences in Mozart should be carefully tapered at the seams. A philosophical approach bodes well for him in an open-air rehearsal in a rural town back home, where he instructs his young musicians, as Stravinsky would conceptualize, to "grab a hold of the space that music inhabits so that it becomes free from time."

A more creative approach works in Los Angeles, where he will often invite his YOLA students to imagine being the "elegant toreador," or the "couple in love." As he is teaching, he is also living the stories with genuine candor and personal immediacy. He never seems to appear imposing or *serious*, but always as the one most eager to have a good time. At the end of a rehearsal he'll close the score and say, "Oh-h, I love music!" That is clearly something he has learned from growing up in El Sistema.

Role Models

"Everyone should be watching this! What a beauty."

A taped concert by the Simón Bolívar Symphony Orchestra of Venezuela in Luzern was being broadcast on TVES, the state-run television network. *Tweets* came from students all over the country. A violinist from Nueva Esparta wrote, "I am watching Angelica play. It's magical."

"Play us an encore," said another student from Maracaibo.

The violin soloist, Angelica Olivo, is a well-known musician among El Sistema students. She is regarded as one of the crown jewels of the national program, and is often seen sitting in the concertmaster's chair; or playing concerts under the direction of such legendary conductors as Claudio Abbado—a mentor of hers. Her musical career is yet to unfold, but at the age of twenty, she is already poised for greater recognition, and stardom, perhaps. She comes from a musical family. At twelve, she auditioned for Francisco del Castillo, the head of the Latin American Academy of Violin in Caracas, and was immediately admitted to his class. At Maestro Abreu's request, she joined the Teresa Carreño Youth Orchestra and quickly gained recognition as a talent of huge potential. "Being a musician is to be special . . . because music pacifies the soul. To make music is the most gratifying of all feelings," she told a national newspaper. And she takes her music very seriously. Her daily routine includes getting in some practice time early, "around 6:30 in the morning." Her orchestra rehearses every day, except on Sundays. "Music has rewarded me with so many good things. I have to keep studying a lot!" she says.

For students like Angelica, playing also means being a role model for hundreds, if not thousands, of other violin students across the country. It can be a huge responsibility. Her accomplishments will fuel the dreams of many fellow young musicians, motivate them, and help them fulfill their own potential. Maestro Abreu himself sees these young performers as the future *national maestros*. "They will have many opportunities to play outside of Venezuela and offers to perform as part of world-renowned orchestras," he told me, "but their heart will always remain with their country and with their own."

This is one of the most compelling aspects of El Sistema. Students can aspire to be a shining example of excellence, not just for art's sake, but for their own country's sake—to become champions of music, and as consequence, ambassadors of national culture.

In many ways, Angelica represents a utopia. She is there to serve as an example and to generate new standards. The students who are practicing the Sibelius *Violin Concerto* or the Beethoven *Romances* won't be just referring to the interpretations of Anne-Sophie Mutter or Julia Fischer. They will also have their own "big sister" to look up to, making it yet another reason to be proud and hopeful of their own dreams in music.

"Tocar y Luchar"

Towards the end of a rehearsal with a youth orchestra in Punto Fijo, a town in the country's northwestern Caribbean coast, the students asked me if we could do the Saint-Saens *Dance Macabre*, just for fun. I said I'd love to play it, but perhaps next time (I hadn't studied that piece yet).

"That's OK," the musicians said, "you don't have to do it perfectly. We'll teach it to you!"

We started the music. I struggled a bit, but it worked. There was no need to worry about having to produce a finished performance. We were conquering the challenge together and that is all that mattered to them.

What did I learn? I learned that I could learn very quickly if I was pushed to the occasion! I also learned that music didn't have to be the formal and scary thing I had been trained to perceive it to be during my conservatory years. These daring musical feats (which can feel as if you're about to jump of a cliff) permeate the pedagogical consciousness of El Sistema.

Alfredo Rugeles, an accomplished Venezuelan conductor and composer, tells a similar story:

"Maestro Abreu will call you one morning, and tell you that *in the afternoon* he would like to have a reading of Mahler's *Seventh Symphony*, although you've never seen the piece! That creates a *struggle* that requires the use of all of your capacities. In my case, it has helped me to refine the process of score reading, which has allowed me to learn more."

In many of the orchestras I worked with in Venezuela, there were sometimes, one or two musicians lacking the technical skill to play the repertoire at an "acceptable" level. It called for an interesting discussion. If you were to make music of the highest caliber, wouldn't you need to have an audition to be sure *every* player had the necessary technique to thrive in the orchestra?

In the US, more often than not, membership in a traditional youth orchestra is contingent upon an audition process. In principle, students would have to have had private lessons for at least two or three years before being admitted to a junior orchestra. Not in El Sistema.

The Venezuelan youth orchestra model is built upon the belief that by inserting an "untrained" child into the orchestra, he will learn to perceive problems as challenges and never as obstacles. A beginner student will learn to learn quickly by observing his peers and melding his sound onto the more advanced players. They don't mind at all because they too were once in those same shoes. But does that mean that the product suffers for it?

Not necessarily, because one has to realize artistry encompasses a much wider process. For in education as the practice of freedom, as Paulo Freire suggests, students must be "their own example in the struggle for their redemption." They should view themselves as "conscious beings who are unfinished, yet in the process of becoming."

And for that same reason, teachers in El Sistema will place their students in more advanced ensembles even when they may not be ready, and constantly remind them to play their music "with the heart" or "with feeling." It is a very romantic notion; but isn't as we've explored here the role of *artistic doingness* to connect, to feel, and to say that which has not been said before? It is through this same context that a child's art, however perfect or imperfect, is humanized and its interpreter brought to a place of transformation.

And it turns the orchestra into a laboratory, where the learning is never contingent upon previous experience or knowledge, but framed upon the construct that every child should find herself in a continuous process of becoming. I think this might be why they often say, *"Tocar y luchar."* "To play *and* to struggle."

CONSTRUCT, DECONSTRUCT

Frank Ghery, the inspired Canadian architect known for his trailblazing work in experimental architecture and design, is a staunch champion of El Sistema. *Pancho*, as Gustavo Dudamel affectionately calls him, often collaborates with the conductor in an artistic capacity. His latest commission was to build stage sets for a production of Mozart's *Don Giovanni* in Los Angeles.

In early March of 2012, it was announced that he would design a new National Center for Music in Barquisimeto. The Minister of Communications reported the news in an official press release. Ghery said that the center would be "inspired by the spirit of Maestro Abreu, Gustavo Dudamel, and the Simón Bolívar Orchestra. My inspiration will come from here, from the people of Venezuela," he said. "It is an emotional commission. The most important thing is to design a concert hall that will foster a relationship between performers and audiences." The design and construction is expected to be completed in three to five years.

Frank Ghery is known for his incursion into *deconstructivist* architecture. The Walt Disney Concert Hall in downtown Los Angeles and the Guggenheim Museum in Bilbao are examples of that work. According to curators from the Museum of Modern Art (MoMa), the "hallmark of deconstructivist architecture is its apparent instability." In practice, deconstructivism is characterized by "stimulating unpredictability and a controlled chaos." On the subject, Philip Johnson and Mark Wigley wrote:

"Though structurally sound, projects seem to be in states of explosion or collapse. Towers are turned over on their sides; bridges are tilted up to become towers; underground elements erupt from the earth and float above the surface; commonplace materials become suddenly exotic. Deconstructivist architecture, however, is not an architecture of decay or demolition. On the contrary, it gains all of its force by . . . proposing instead that flaws are intrinsic to the structure."

Ultimately, Ghery believes that his architecture will be as successful as its ability to invite a space of unity in which the user may bring "his baggage, his program, and interact with it to accommodate his needs," he explains. This is a fascinating artistic concept and one that could also be readily applied to describe the pedagogical *ethos* of El Sistema. Unpredictability and chaos are if anything, two of the most discerning realities of the program. Interestingly enough, those same two make a lot of music educators outside of Venezuela very nervous.

People often ask me if there are method books or guidelines available from "the source" for building El Sistema-inspired programs. It is a valid question, and it is only natural that people would ask, since the term El Sistema, which translates into "the system," literally conveys an expectation of there being a manual or user's guide. To this day, there have been remarkable contributions by my colleagues and other practitioners who, in an effort to bring clarity and structure to the work, have outlined various "principles" or "elements" of El Sistema, and in the interim have found practical solutions to addressing the question. But any questions pertaining to El Sistema should only be addressed by posing more questions. It cannot be underestimated that flexibility and creativity are of utmost importance here.

Josbel Puche, the director of Núcleo *La Rinconada* in Caracas is known for her work as an advocate of the "paper orchestra," a concept that grew out of instrument scarcity rather than pedagogical intent. The idea consists of building *papier maché* string instruments from scratch. An entire community of teachers, students, and families will convene to build and decorate them giving each instrument a unique personality. Once in hand, musical exercises are built upon concepts leading to actual orchestra rehearsals. How to hold the bow, care for the instrument, follow the conductor, and interact with their peers are all lessons that can be learned throughout the process, one that may last on average about four to six weeks or until their real instruments arrive!

I asked her if she had developed her own method book to share with others. "We don't write anything down. We create every single day," she said. Traditional approaches to pedagogy dictate elaborate lesson plans, faithful adherence to established method books, and *rules*. This is not the case in Venezuela. As with technology, pedagogy becomes obsolete as soon as it has been unpacked.

Maestro Abreu is always reluctant to call his own program a system. "It is an anti-system," he says. The system has evolved through a process of constant trial-and-error and thrives through an active *listening* to the needs of those who are to be served.

El Sistema's authenticity, if one were to make such a claim, wouldn't derive upon any specific methods or strict pedagogies, but on its flexibility to be constructed, deconstructed, and then constructed again. Yes, there is in Venezuela certain uniformity in the way youngsters are taught, the repertoire that is chosen, even the bowings and fingerings used on string parts. That same uniformity allows students to incorporate quickly and readily into any other orchestra within El Sistema. The point is that the *whole* Sistema should feel like one big orchestra. And although every musical community can be "different," they will all share a homogeneous artistic consciousness. Might there be a "system" after all? Perhaps, but I would be hesitant to call it as such.

Having lived with El Sistema and reflected upon the work of Paulo Freire, an academic whose teachings I feel to be very much in tune with El Sistema's dynamics of social transformation, I am inclined to propose that the system, at its core, is much less prescriptive and more dialogical. Maestro Abreu, who seldom describes it, much less defines it, spoke to a journalist from *The Guardian* and said that it may operate more like "a concept regarding the function of music within society."

The pedagogy of El Sistema is grounded on enacting dialogues of participation between teachers, students, and the community-at-large. Its praxis is the beneficiaries' own praxis. A standardized method cannot be imposed because the same would impede carrying out its mission. The beneficiary must find, of his own accord, meaning for his own experience, reflect upon it, and guide his own conscious transformation. The "system" itself cannot do this for him, nor prescribe a magic antidote to alleviate his needs. It is through the practice of music that he finds a way to *awaken* his "critical conscience," which will inevitably guide him to fulfill his own material and/or spiritual liberation.

The orchestra is a generous space for learning, reflection, and growth. In entering such a dynamic edifice of musical exchange, which can only be built through a *relentless* seeking of excellence and beauty, a student will come to embrace the value of his contributions and more ample reasons to define himself as an individual who probes for the advancement and renewal of his condition. Because to play *also* means to strive. That is the revolutionary nature of the program. (The thoroughly descriptive yet succinct words of American poet Maya Angelou seem to fit seamlessly with the notion of students achieving *transformations* through self-reliance and a persevering spirit: "Nothing will work unless you do.")

In light of the *Piagetian* constructivist theory of learning (where participants "raise their own questions, construct their own models, pursue autonomy, and empowerment"), El Sistema can be seen as a malleable space for the breeding of new pedagogical tools and ideas through the *synthesis* of a multitude of converging perspectives.

These perspectives are key to the strength and growth of the overall program, as national and guest teachers will often travel around the country and disseminate new information, practices, and ideas; and yet, El Sistema's original *raison d'être* will remain intact. One could argue that yielding to external influences (going off script) would be a hurdle to the success of any program, however, many of times El Sistema music directors would invite the Fellows to lead sessions or rehearsals with orchestras and choirs immediately after our arrival at the núcleos. It was natural to deviate from the norm: to quickly arrange an additional rehearsal, work on an entirely different repertoire, or invite a conductor to lead an ensemble in concert—the day of the concert! All in benefit of the greater whole.

Anyone seeking to replicate El Sistema must not strive to subtract from it, but add to it with their own ideas and experiences; or in the words of Maxine Greene, by "using their own lives, knowledge, and explorations as elements within the curriculum." It is also of utmost importance that educators in El Sistema and elsewhere be prepared to think "with their students, and not for them, or without them," as Greene would also attest. As moderators of a process of transformative education, teachers are called upon to be genuinely engaged with their students, anticipating and meeting their needs synergistically, so that education becomes more of a process of inquiry and less of a system of best practices.

If there is something I've learned in Venezuela about program building it is that everyone must learn to develop their own "system" within the scope of their own means and aptitudes. And while doing so, strive to find ways to incorporate it into the fabric of their very own communities. And as Maestro Abreu challenges us, dare to "create some chaos that will eventually lead to order." That is how it has been done for over 37 years.

TRAINING A NEW GENERATION

There aren't always enough teachers to meet the growing demands of El Sistema in Venezuela, but surely, their leaders always find creative ways to attend to their students. It is one of the many virtues of the "system" to make ends meet with the best of available resources.

As we explored the challenges of sustaining and expanding the El Sistema *movement* in Venezuela, Rodrigo Cedeño, the twenty something academic director for the rural state of Guárico, pulled out a piece of paper to describe expansion plans for his region. He drew his home state's map, placing markers on existing núcleos. "Here's Valle de la Pascua, Tucupido, and Zaraza; and there are six more around this area, nine total!" he said. "We need to grow, but we must do so organically."

He then went on to describe how they would build satellite sites or *modulos* around them, focusing on bringing choirs and orchestras to schools and other unconventional sites such as a trash dump (where some school children also work). "We can build three additional sites around this núcleo. We can hire our best students to teach, but we must train them first!" The Fellows sitting around the dinner table have become very enthused. The young leader's passion is rubbing off. Another map is drawn up. It looks like the United States!

Each Fellow has stamped where their future programs will be located, drawing up satellite sites, connecting dots among existing programs, and envisioning a *movement*. It is an exciting line up of initiatives. Stephanie Hsu will lead Yakima Música en Acción, an El Sistema-inspired program in Washington State's Yakima Valley. She will team up with an existing human services and economic development organization to work with children of migrant families from Central and South America. Alysia Lee will serve as the Artistic Director of Sister Cities Girlchoir, a choral program to provide a safe space for at-risk girls to develop habits of healthy and ethical living in Camden and Philadelphia. One of her dreams is to prepare the girls to sing Vivaldi's *Gloria* and take them to the World Choir Games. Ben Fuller is starting the Queen City Music Project in his hometown city of Charlotte.

Albert Oppenheimer is joining the YOURS Project, an orchestral based program in Chicago, where he hopes to develop composition and improvisation as teaching tools. Aisha Bowden, a former Washington D.C. school teacher, will team up with Dantes Rameau, the stalwart founder of the El Sistema-inspired Atlanta Music Project to begin a brand new choral program, which will use music as a "pathway to success" for hundreds of children throughout the city. It is just the beginning of a long journey ahead of us. Moving forward, each of us will envision meaningful opportunities to make a difference.

El Sistema leaders in Venezuela are well aware that in order to grow responsibly, they must continually train new teachers. El Sistema's plans for national growth in Venezuela are extremely ambitious. They aspire to serve one million children by the year 2020. Maestro Abreu often insists that "culture for the poor cannot be a poor culture." This also means that the poorest of children should have the best musical instruments *and* teachers. (In Caracas, plans are underway for the construction and development of the *Centro de Capacitación Docente*, a state-of-the-art national center for teacher training.)

In the United States, El Sistema-inspired leaders have also taken note and are actively involved in helping advance artistic and leadership training opportunities for individuals who aspire to be "messengers of music and of the social mission of art." My colleague Anne Fitzgibbon has built the El Sistema-inspired *Harmony Program* around the idea of training new teaching corps. Hiring young college students and providing them with professional development opportunities guides the philosophy of her work. In Los Angeles, *YOLA*, Gustavo Dudamel's signature program, will serve as a laboratory for developing El Sistema-inspired teaching practices in collaboration with the Longy School of Music of Bard College's newly minted Master of Arts in Teaching program.

In Baltimore, Daniel Trahey, the artistic director of *Orchkids*, an El Sistema-inspired program of the Baltimore Symphony Orchestra, will begin training new teachers as part of a post-graduate entrepreneurship and musician-ship certificate program at the University of Maryland. My colleague Stanford Thompson, the founder of *Play-on, Philly*! is heading an effort to train El Sistema-inspired leaders and musicians through regional symposiums. I am developing curricula and frameworks for teaching and learning geared to help develop the artistic and pro-grammatic capacities of both emerging and established El Sistema-inspired initiatives. Our combined efforts will help bring a *social action* focus to the forefront of peda-gogical thinking and practice in a wide variety of settings. These will be important contributions to the thriving music education ecosystem in the United States and beyond.

As the conversation carries well beyond midnight, the Fellows have begun to think about recruiting fellow teachers for their own programs. What elements should be part of their training? What strengths and attributes should they bring to the núcleos? The first virtue that comes to my mind is a heart filled with hope.

Place No Limits

Mira cuántas brillan,
mira cuántas brillan,
en la inmensidad.

Una es tuya, niño,
una es tuya, niño,
y de nadie más.

A group of children are singing in two-part harmony—
it's a song about *reaching for the stars*. "Look at how they
shine; one of them is yours, and only yours." The poignant lyrics seem to have become the children's own. Their
teacher, a recent college graduate, is leading the music.
She is conducting with a lovely expression. She is also
singing along to support the voices of the small children
who sometimes fall out of tune. Some of them are reading
the score, but most of them already know it by heart. It
really doesn't matter to them whether they've hit all the
right notes or not. They seem to be enraptured in the

moment: closing their eyes as to savor the soulful music. To their right is another group of children wearing white gloves. They are not singing, but their eyes are shining.

As the chorus starts again, they lift their arms up in the air. It is as if they are *conducting* the music themselves, accentuating every nuance with a turn of the wrist or a folding of the arms. Their carefully choreographed gestures ebb and flow with gleaming hope. It is a beautiful spectacle. They are sculpting the sound with elegant eloquence. But they cannot hear it. They are deaf.

We are asked to join the "White Hands" choir for their next piece. "Come on; put the *Flipcams* and notepads away. It's time to make music," says their impassioned teacher. "Come experience what our children experience!" Still in awe of their performance, we proceed to join the choir. As we line up as part of the ensemble, the children introduce themselves in sign language. Their repertoire includes the national anthem, folk songs, as well as other classical masterworks, including their signature piece, John Rutter's Christmas setting of the *Ave Maria.*

"As soon as the music begins, look at my eyes, and follow me," our conductor instructs us. She begins with gentle motions, up and to the side. Her hands are also very expressive. Then quick movements follow and it's hard to keep up. As a piano accompaniment plays a transition, she says, "As you can see, it's much harder than it looks. You have a long way to go! We are teaching a new vocabulary. Our children can sing too!" It is a strenuous exercise, but the children have developed the endurance to perform with ease. There is a great level of technique involved. It is all about engaging with the feeling of movement, and the activity takes on a larger meaning when it is done as a group.

The children *sing* through signing and by integrating corporal gestures to describe the meaning of the music. Their gestures must flow into each other with exact rhythmic precision. We are mirroring the teacher's movements, and because she is facing us, she is performing in reverse motion, adding another degree of virtuosity to the mix. As we finish the piece, we all applaud in silence by waving our hands up in the air. There are hugs and smiles exchanged. And we are reminded, yet again, that in a spirit of generosity learning knows no limits.

Coda

April 3, 2012

I remember, vividly, the day that I decided to study music. *I wanted to be an artist.* As a child, I didn't know what that meant, but I knew how it sounded. I would listen to Leonard Bernstein's recordings of the Beethoven symphonies for hours on end. Somewhere, I heard that if you studied piano, you could *play* the sounds of an orchestra. So I decided to take lessons. I remember having to sign a contract at the local community arts school—literally. This simple and yet daunting document stipulated that I would commit to attending lessons, practicing at home, and dedicating the effort into producing "results of artistic value."

Of course, I quickly realized that music was *not* easy. And that it would take a while to reproduce the sounds that were so endearing to me. Nonetheless, a meaningful journey in music began, right then. My first piano teacher wasn't a world-renowned artist or pedagogue, but he instilled in me a sense of purpose—the idea that any student, even at the initial stages of learning, should feel that his life in music and the arts is important. My parents lovingly encouraged me to pursue my goals. My community applauded my efforts. I was lucky to have such wonderful mentors and opportunities growing up.

All children should have an opportunity to experience the power of music as it will add tremendous value to their lives. They will come to know beauty in profound ways, but most importantly, come to imagine themselves as purveyors of that same virtue. In Venezuela, Maestro Abreu has made sure that every child who aspires to a life in music will have the opportunity to sing and to play—and to dream. El Sistema has made it a social right. "For Venezuelans, music education is now a constitutional and legal right," he says.

One of the most memorable impressions of my journey in Venezuela has been the sheer fact that every child in an orchestra or choir feels his contributions as important. When children play, they come to realize that they are part of something that really matters. Their communities will applaud and recognize them, their parents will listen to them practice at home, and their teachers will always encourage them to strive and reach for higher goals. Such a space of generosity can only breed the kind of opportunities that will lead them to envision more productive lives. Indeed, "translating our humanness to its maximum dimension" through the practice of music; and while seeking to harmonize instruments and voices in and within the experience of the aesthetic, begets a new heightened self-awareness to elevate and dignify the human spirit. "The choirs and orchestras prepare the spirit for a more pleasing life, they imprint a sense of joy and hope, and broaden the horizons," the maestro explains.

In an orchestra, as musicians come together to learn from each other, they expand the narrow perception of art as an entity of exclusivity. They re-imagine music, fitting it to their own broader social construct, that of a new reality stemming from both an aesthetic purpose and social need. This duality of artistic motivation creates the kind of musical accomplishments that captivate the imagination. In being one with music and community artistry thrives and evolves.

Beyond a musical aesthetic, pioneering pedagogy, or a cultural phenomenon, El Sistema should always be seen as a window into the realm of the possible. A new space where all youngsters, families, and communities can come together to experience the values of music in nurturing and non-competitive environments; and where educators envision their profession as an instrument to encourage meaningful social transformations. El Sistema's foremost goal is not to produce instrumental virtuosos, but rather, citizens of virtue—young people empowered with new tools and perspectives to help them overcome the challenges of life.

In Caracas, during our meeting with Maestro Abreu, our visionary host, bustling with energetic impetus and eager to hear the stories of our journey, began by telling us that he was very interested to hear a perspective on how El Sistema could be improved. "What have you seen on the ground that we can further perfect? What can we learn?" he asked.

The Fellows spoke about the experiences that had the most profound impact on our own learning and development as socially conscious artists. My colleague Stephanie Hsu spoke of her experience working with deaf children in the city of Coro. While helping prepare Schubert's *Ave Maria*, Maryelanis, a young choral teacher instructed her: "You asked me before, 'What do you need to know to do this work well?' Everything that you do, think, and feel is transmitted through your eyes." For a moment, I was reminded again of the maestro's teaching philosophy—El Sistema is about realizing a new meaning behind the threads of human connections, uncovering the "invisible transmitted unseen through music."

Alysia Lee drew a parallel to her early *amateur* life remembering how excited she always was to be at every teen gospel choir rehearsal. She touched upon the notion of amateurism as a space of opportunity. "The etymological root for the word amateur is *"ama"* or "to love," she said. "A final amateur product may lack accuracy, but the process and the preparation are filled with love. Therein lies the El Sistema paradigm!"

Albert Oppenheimer discovered that composers were "virtually everywhere in El Sistema," but that "a structure was still needed to nurture them."

Aisha Bowden celebrated the "beauty and infectious spirit of the Venezuelan people."

Avi Mehta, a fellow conductor, stood and shared how El Sistema has mustered the art of unconditional giving where "the goals and needs of the collective always take precedence over the needs of the individual."

David France reflected upon his experiences working in *Las Panelas*, seeing how his students "progressed so quickly."

Jennifer Kessler, a French horn player, spoke about being in Soroco and in the midst of a landscape of poverty, teaching and learning alongside a little cellist who was planting seeds "that would bear him fruits of possibility."

Julie Davis recalled the times the Fellows would travel together, hoping to uncover "new treasures" as we went along.

Ben Fuller reiterated the fact, that indeed, El Sistema is "very hard work."

I also spoke to the maestro about the experience of working with his orchestras. We exchanged ideas for thinking about the arts in new and innovative ways. We explored how music can be best positioned as a social and participatory art to be shared generously in and through communities. We touched upon plans for future collaborations and opportunities. Our friendships will last for a lifetime. And as the Venezuelans would say, we are now part of a "family dedicated to music and to bringing hope."

After 37 years of incessant servant leadership, the maestro feels that it is just the beginning. There are more horizons to explore, higher goals to reach, more music to share. The overarching vision: to expand the philosophy of El Sistema into countries outside of Venezuela, to unite people through the musical arts, and to place *beauty* at the heart of every community. Bolivia Bottome couldn't agree more, "Our big vision is to make this a world project. We believe this is an experience that every youngster should have," she told us, "not necessarily to become a musician, but as a life experience."

Maestro Abreu envisions a world filled with orchestras. "Everyday life should be expressed through music," he says. This ideal may also lead us to envision our art as a vehicle for advancing peace—music as an instrument to balance and recognize the voices of those in need of the spiritual comfort that only artistic endeavors can bring. An enduring message of hope is ever-present in the ethos of El Sistema. It is a powerful music-making because it stems from deep aspirations to realize more dignified lives, and from the pride that emanates from communities as they see themselves being *transformed* through their art. In the twenty-first century, the work of El Sistema is opening up new ways of thinking about the arts and its purpose in society. I am energized and hopeful about the future of music and education in our time.

A TED PRIZE SPEECH

Maestro Abreu's TED Prize Speech was given in February of 2009 to an audience in Long Beach, California, via recorded and live telecast from Caracas. It is a remarkable testament to his artistic vision. The discourse positions the maestro as a consummate teacher, borrowing the words of Maxine Greene, who has become "conscious of his own consciousness."

His ability to embrace visionary ideals with an absolute conviction to act upon them makes his words *resonate* with a sublime profundity. The speech was also one of my entry points into the dialectic of El Sistema. It spoke to my own consciousness, answering a long series of questions that as an artist I had deep within me, but had not found a way to articulate yet.

How may the arts be made manifest in the spirit of community? How do we articulate an art that is more generous, more genuine, and at the service of society? How do we design new experiences for musicians and audiences as active participants of beauty?

In an effort to spread "ideas worth sharing," I include an unabridged transcript of the speech. More than half a million people around the globe have already heard this message via TED.com. I hope that you'll be inspired by the speech and revisit it often.

"My dear friends, ladies and gentlemen: I am overjoyed today at being awarded the TED Prize on behalf of all the distinguished music teachers, artists, and educators from Venezuela who have selflessly and loyally accompanied me for 35 years in founding, growing, and developing the National System of Youth and Children's Orchestras and Choirs of Venezuela.

Since I was a boy, in my early childhood, I always wanted to be a musician, and, thank God, I made it. From my teachers, my family, and my community, I had all the necessary support to become a musician. All my life I've dreamed that all Venezuelan children have the same opportunity that I had. From that desire and from my heart stemmed the idea to make music a deep and global reality for my country.

From the very first rehearsal, I saw the bright future ahead, because the rehearsal meant a great challenge to me. I had received a donation of 50 music stands to be used by 100 boys in that rehearsal. When I arrived at the rehearsal, only eleven kids had shown up, and I said to myself, "Do I close the program or multiply these kids?" I decided to face the challenge, and on that same night, I promised those eleven children I'd turn our orchestra into one of the *leading* orchestras in the world. Two months ago, I remembered that promise I made, when a distinguished English critic published an article in the *London Times*, asking who could be the winner of the *Orchestra World Cup*. He mentioned four great world orchestras, and the fifth one was Venezuela's Youth Symphony Orchestra. Today we can say that art in Latin America is no longer a monopoly of elites and that it has become a social right, a right for all the people.

During the recent tour by the Simón Bolívar Youth Orchestra of Venezuela of the U.S. and Europe, we saw how our music moved young audiences to the bottom of their souls, how children and adolescents rushed up to the stage to receive the jackets from our musicians, how the standing ovations, sometimes 30 minutes long, seemed to last forever, and how the public, after the concert was over, would go into the streets to greet our young people in triumph. This meant not only an artistic triumph, but also a profound emotional sympathy between the public of the most advanced nations of the world and the musical youth of Latin America, as seen in Venezuela, giving these audiences a message of music, vitality, energy, enthusiasm, and strength.

In its essence, the orchestra and the choir are much more than artistic structures. They are examples and schools of social life, because to sing and to play together means to intimately coexist toward perfection and excellence, following a strict discipline of organization and coordination in order to seek the harmonic interdependence of voices and instruments. That's how they build a spirit of solidarity and fraternity among them, develop their self-esteem, and foster the ethical and aesthetical values related to the music in all its senses. This is why music is immensely important in the awakening of sensibility, in the forging of values, and in the training of youngsters to teach other kids.

Each teenager and child in El Sistema has his own story, and they are all important and of great significance to me. Let me mention the case of Edicson Ruiz. He is a boy from a parish in Caracas who passionately attended to his double bass lessons at the San Agustin's Junior Orchestra. With his effort; and the support of his mother, his family, and his community, he became a principal member in the double bass section of the Berlin Philharmonic Orchestra. We have another well-known case—Gustavo Dudamel. He started as a boy member of the children's orchestra in his hometown, Barquisimeto. There, he grew as a violinist and as a conductor. He became the conductor of Venezuela's youth orchestras, and today conducts the world's *greatest* orchestras. He is the musical director of the Los Angeles Philharmonic, and is still the overall leader of Venezuela's youth orchestras. He was the conductor of the Gothenburg Symphony Orchestra, and he's an unbeatable example for young musicians in Latin America and the world.

The structure of El Sistema is based on a new and flexible managing style adapted to the features of each community and region, and today attends to 300,000 children of the lower and middle-class all over Venezuela. It's a program of social rescue and deep cultural transformation designed to serve the entire Venezuelan society with absolutely no distinctions whatsoever, but emphasizing on the vulnerable and endangered social groups.

The effect of El Sistema is felt in three fundamental circles—in the personal/social circle, in the family circle, and in the community. In the personal/social circle, the children in the orchestras and choirs develop their intellectual and emotional side. The music becomes a source for developing the dimensions of the human being, thus elevating the spirit and leading man to a full development of his personality. So, the emotional and intellectual profits are huge: the acquisition of leadership, teaching and training principles, the sense of commitment, responsibility, generosity and dedication to others, and the individual contribution to achieve great collective goals. All this leads to the development of self-esteem and confidence.

Mother Teresa of Calcutta insisted on something that always impressed me—the most miserable and tragic thing about poverty is not the lack of bread or roof, but the feeling of being no-one, the feeling of not being anyone, the lack of identification, the lack of public esteem. That's why the child's development in the orchestra and the choir provides him with a *noble* identity and makes him a role model for his family and community. It makes him a better student at school because it inspires in him a sense of responsibility, perseverance, and punctuality that will greatly help him at school.

Within the family, the parents' support is unconditional. The child becomes a role model to both his parents, and this is very important for a poor child. Once the child discovers he is important for his family, he begins to seek new ways of improving himself and his community. He also *hopes* for social and economic improvements for his own family. All this makes up a constructive and ascending social dynamic. The large majority of our children belong, as I already mentioned, to the most vulnerable strata of the Venezuelan population. That encourages them to embrace new dreams, new goals, and progress in the various opportunities that music has to offer.

Finally, in the circle of the community, the orchestras prove to be the creative spaces of culture and sources of exchange and new meanings. The spontaneity music has excludes it as a luxury item and makes it a patrimony of society. It's what makes a child play a violin at home, while his father works in his carpentry. It's what makes a little girl play the clarinet at home, while her mother does the housework. The idea is that the families join with pride and joy in the activities of the orchestras and the choirs their children belong to. The huge spiritual world that music produces in itself, which also lies within itself, ends up overcoming material poverty. From the minute a child is taught how to play an instrument, he's no longer poor. He becomes a child in progress heading for a professional level of action, who'll later become a full citizen. Needless to say that music is the number one prevention against prostitution, violence, bad habits, and everything degrading in the life of a child.

A few years ago, historian Arnold Toynbee said that the world was suffering a huge spiritual crisis. Not an economic or social crisis, but a spiritual one. I believe that to confront such a crisis, only art and religion can give proper answers to humanity, to mankind's deepest aspirations, and to the historic demands of our times. Education being the synthesis of wisdom and knowledge, it's the means to strive for a more perfect, more aware, more noble, and more just society.

With passion and enthusiasm we pay profound respects to TED for its outstanding humanism, the scope of its principles, and for its open and generous promotion of ethical values in youth. We hope that TED can contribute in a full and fundamental way to the building of this new era in the teaching of music, in which the social, communal, spiritual, and vindicatory aims of the child and the adolescent become a beacon and a goal for a vast social mission. No longer putting society at the service of art, and much less at the services of monopolies of the elite, but instead art at the service of society, at the service of the weakest, at the service of the children, at the service of the sick, at the service of the vulnerable, and at the service of all those who cry for vindication through the spirit of their human condition and the raising up of their dignity.

Here is my TED Prize wish—I wish that you help to create and document a special training program for 50 gifted young musicians passionate about their art and social justice and dedicated to bringing El Sistema to the United States and other countries. Thank you very much."

BIBLIOGRAPHY

Abreu, J. A. (2001, December 7). José Antonio Abreu: THE RIGHT LIVELIHOOD AWARDS 2001. Speech presented at Awards Ceremony, Stockholm.

————.(2008, February 26). José Antonio Abreu's acceptance speech of the Venezuelan branch of B'nai B'rith's Human Rights Award. Speech presented at Awards Ceremony, Caracas.

————.(2009, February 26). José Antonio Abreu on Kids Transformed by Music. Speech presented at TED Prize Presentation in Telecast, Long Beach, California.

————.(2010, April 4). The Abreu (Sistema) Fellows Meet with José Antonio Abreu. Lecture presented at Abreu (Sistema) Fellows Venezuela Residency 2010, Caracas.

————.(2012, April 3). The Sistema Fellows Meet with José Antonio Abreu. Lecture presented at Sistema Fellows Venezuela Residency 2012, Caracas.

Arvelo, A. (Director). (2006). Tocar y Luchar [Motion picture on DVD]. FESNOJIV, Explorart Films, CNAC, and CONAC.

Bohun, S. (Director). (n.d.). Mata Tigre: Change through Music in Venezuela: El Sistema FESNOJIV [Video]. Stefan Bohun. Retrieved from http://documentary.net/

Booth, E. (2010). El Sistema's Open Secrets. Teaching Artist Journal, 9(1).

Borzacchini, C. (2005). Venezuela bursting with orchestras. [Caracas]: Banco del Caribe.

Bottome, B. (2012, April 2). What is your big vision? [Interview by A. Bowden]. Retrieved from http://youtu.be/OH7qZNI8LrI

Building the Brain's "Air Traffic Control" System: How early experiences shape the development of executive function (Working paper No. 11). (2011). Retrieved http://developingchild.harvard.edu/

Burton-Hill, C. (2012, June 14). José Antonio Abreu on Venezuela's El Sistema miracle. The Guardian.

Chavarria, M. (2012, June 19). Gustavo Dudamel: No tengo tiempo para poder sentirme estrella del rock. La Vanguardia.

Csikszentmihalyi, M., & Csikszentmihalyi, I. S. (1988). Optimal experience: Psychological studies of flow in consciousness. Cambridge: Cambridge University Press.

Cuesta, J. (n.d.). Iadb.org (Rep. No. PR 3161). Retrieved March/April, 2012, from Inter-American Development Bank website: http://idbdocs.iadb.org/

Davis, J. (2012, April 27). Better lives through music [Web log post]. Retrieved from http://www.tedprize.org/

Dewey, J. (1938). Logic, the theory of inquiry,. New York: H. Holt and Company.

Elster, R. (2012, March 1). We have eternal forgiveness... [Interview by A. Bowden]. Retrieved from http://youtu.be/FJvhhPPlCKI

Emanuel, M., & Sharp, D. (1980). Contemporary architects. New York: St. Martin's Press.

Freire, P. (2000). Pedagogy of the oppressed. New York: Continuum.

Gardner, H. (2011). Truth, Beauty, and Goodness Reframed: Educating for the Virtues in the 21st Century. New York: Basic Books.

Giménez, J. (2012, March 5). The Genesis of El Sistema [Personal interview].

González-Fuentes, J. A. (2008, July 3). Gustavo Dudamel y la Orquesta Sinfónica Simón Bolívar montan una Fiesta [Review of FIESTA (DG)]. El Pulso De La Bruma.

Greene, M. (1972). Curriculum and Consciousness. Teachers College Record, 73(2), 253-270.

————.(1977). Toward wide-awakeness: An Argument for the Arts and Humanities in Education. Teachers College Record, 79, 119-125.

————.(1995). Releasing the Imagination: Essay; on Education, the Arts, and Social Change. San Francisco: Jossey-Bass.

Guerrero, R. (2012, March 1). Conversations on El Sistema [Personal interview].

Gustavo Dudamel conducts Beethoven [Video]. (2006). Deutsche Grammophon. Retrieved March 15, 2012, from http://youtu.be/THTpisVKto8

Hernández, T. (2012, March 30). On Conducting and Teaching [Personal interview].

Hernández-Estrada, J. L. (Trans.). (2009, May 26). Sueña con ser una gran solista. El Nacional.

Ho, W. (n.d.). Constructivism and Learning [Scholarly project]. Retrieved from http://www.personal.psu.edu/

Hsu, S. (2012, March 9). Bendiciones en Barquisimeto [Web log post]. Retrieved from
http://respiriting.wordpress.com/

Kessler, J. (2012, April 26). Growing Out of Poverty, Violin in Hand [Web log post]. Retrieved from
http://www.tedprize.org/

Lee, A. (2012, May 3). Sistema Choirs: Collaboration, Excellence & Passion [Web log post]. Retrieved from
http://www.tedprize.org/

Locke, E. A., & Latham, G. P. (1990). A theory of goal setting & task performance. Englewood Cliffs, NJ: Prentice Hall.

Lubow, A. (2007, October 27). Conductor of the People. New York Times.

Mendez, E. (2012, March 1). The Sistema Fellows Meet with Eduardo Mendez. Lecture presented at Sistema Fellows Venezuela Residency 2012, Caracas.

Mendoza, F., Mendez, E., & Guerrero, R. (2012, January 31). TAS Symposium: Voices from Venezuela. Lecture presented at Take a Stand Conference 2012, Los Angeles.

Meyer, L. (1961). Meaning and Emotion in Music. Chicago: University of Chicago Press.

Molina, I. (2012, March 1). You want to work with whom? [Interview by D. France]. Retrieved from
http://youtu.be/92PnTGE7uq8

Mora-Brito, D. (2011). "Between Social Harmony and Political Dissonance: The institutional and policy-based intricacies of the Venezuelan System of Children and Youth Orchestras." (Master's thesis, University of Texas at Austin, 2011). Austin: University of Texas.

Oppenheimer, A. (2012, April 30). Composition in El Sistema [Web log post]. Retrieved from http://www.tedprize.org/

Aesthetics of Generosity

Oursler, R. D. (1969). The effect of Pestalozzian theory and practice on music education in the United States between 1850 and 1900.

Pradas, M. (2008, April 13). Maestro José Antonio Abreu: Con la formación estética debemos desarrollar éticamente la sociedad [Web log post]. Retrieved from http://azulfortaleza.blogspot.mx/

Putnam, R. D. (1995). Bowling Alone: America's Declining Social Capital. Journal of Democracy, 6(1), 65-78.

Rabinowitch, T. (2012, June 13). Music of Kindness: Playing Together Strengthens Empathy in Children [Scholarly project]. In Research News. Retrieved from http://www.cam.ac.uk/research/news/

Ramos, M. E. (2007). Diálogos con el Arte: Entrevistas 1976-2007. Caracas: Equinoccio.

Rodriguez, Oro, Agencia Venezolana de Noticias. (n.d.). Arquitecto canadiense Frank Ghery diseñará sede del Sistema de Orquestas en Lara [Press release].

Sanchez, F. (2007). El Sistema Nacional para las Orquestas Juveniles e Infantiles: La Nueva Educación Musical de Venezuela. Revista Da ABEM, 18.

Schatt, M. (2011). Achievement Motivation and the Adolescent Musician: A Synthesis of the Literature. RIME, 9(1).

Schleuter, S. L. (1984). A sound approach to teaching instrumentalists: An application of content and learning sequences. Kent, OH: Kent State University Press.

Smaczny, P., & Stodtmeir, M. (Directors). (2009). El Sistema: Music to Change Life [Motion picture on DVD]. Euroarts Music.

Wakin, D. J. (2012, February 16). Fighting Poverty, Armed With Violins. New York Times, p. C1.

Weber, M. (1962). Basic concepts in sociology. New York: Philosophical Library.

Wenger, E. (1998). Communities of practice: Learning, meaning, and identity. Cambridge, U.K.: Cambridge University Press.

Wigley, M., & Johnson, P. (1988). Deconstructivist architecture [Pamphlet]. New York, NY: MoMA.

Witkowski, C. (2010, April 29). 8-15 Year Olds Take on the Titan [Web log post]. Retrieved from http://cwabreufellows.wordpress.com/

Zak, P. J., Kurzban, R., & Matzner, W. T. (2004). The Neurobiology of Trust. Annals of the New York Academy of Sciences, 1032(1), 224-227.

PHOTOGRAPHS

The Fellows, faculty, and friends meet with José Antonio Abreu and Gustavo Dudamel at La Sede, Caracas. (NEC)

Young musicians rehearse at Núcleo Las Panelas, Coro.

Choristers sing folk songs, Mahomito.

Young percussionists in an open-air lesson, Caracas.

A Reading of Tchaikovsky's *Fourth Symphony*, Caracas.

Wind sectional rehearsal at Núcleo La Sarría, Caracas.

Viola Masterclass! con la Maestra Hsu, Coro. (S. Hsu)

José Luis Hernández-Estrada

A group of children perform at a rural school, Valle de la Pascua.

Playing and dancing to folk music, Calabozo.

Young percussionist at Núcleo Santa Rosa, Barquisimeto.

"Daily life should be expressed through music." A family heads home with a cello and *cuatro* in hand, Tucupido.

Gustavo Dudamel and the *Bolívars* at La Sede, Caracas.

Choir members perform with "Tocar y Luchar" Medallions at
Núcleo Montalbán, Caracas.

The 2011-2012 Sistema Fellows with Maestro Abreu. (NEC)

The Fellows share with José Antonio Abreu in his office at
Parque Central, Caracas. (NEC)

ABOUT THE AUTHOR

José Luis is an American-born Mexican conductor, educator, and scholar. He gave his first performance at the age of ten performing Haydn's *Piano Concerto* with orchestra—and fell in love with music. A graduate of the Sistema Fellows program at the New England Conservatory, he earned performance degrees from Texas Christian University and the University of Texas Pan-American. He was a Conducting Fellow of *The Conductors Institute* at Bard College Conservatory of Music and also received musical training at the Conservatori del Liceu in Barcelona. He has been invited to work with youth and professional orchestras throughout the Americas including many El Sistema Youth Orchestras in Venezuela; the LA Philharmonic's YOLA, the Hartford Symphony Orchestra, and the *Orquesta Filarmónica de la UNAM*. A passionate advocate for music education and the arts, he founded one of Mexico's largest El Sistema-inspired programs. He served on the faculty of the Austin Chamber Music Center and the Van Cliburn Foundation. An engaging public speaker, he has also participated as a presenter at the Harvard Center for Public Leadership, the *Take a Stand* Symposium, and the League of American Orchestras National Conference. His writings on music education have been featured on TED.com, *The Ensemble*, and *Symphony Now*. He enjoys traveling, perusing modern art, and playing chamber music. This is his first book.

Meeting Maestro Abreu, Los Angeles. (E. Kibler-Vermaas)

Made in the USA
Charleston, SC
27 December 2012